Artificial Intelligence, and Civilization

Artificial intelligence is shaking up economies around the world as well as society at large and is predicted to be either the best or the worst thing to happen to humanity. This book looks at what exactly artificial intelligence is, how it can be classified, how it differentiates from other concepts such as machine learning, big data, and the internet-of-things, and how it has evolved and might evolve over time.

Providing a clear and unbiased picture of artificial intelligence, the book provides critical analyses of the advantages and disadvantages, opportunities and threats of AI progress for business and civilization. Solutions and possible directions of how humanity might deal with rapid development and evolutions will be given and discussed, and regulation, employment, ethics, education, and international cooperation will be considered. Unlike existing literature, this book provides a comprehensive overview of AI based on detailed analysis and insight. Finally, several real-life examples from various sectors and industries, including for-profit organizations, higher education, and government, will substantiate and illustrate the presented concepts, classifications, and discussions.

This book is of interest to researchers, educators, students, and practitioners alike who desire to understand AI in its broad lines and discover the latest research and studies within the field.

Andreas Kaplan is Professor and Dean of ESCP Business School Paris, Sorbonne Alliance. His research focuses on decrypting the digital world, mainly artificial intelligence and social media.

Routledge Focus on Business and Management

The fields of business and management have grown exponentially as areas of research and education. This growth presents challenges for readers trying to keep up with the latest important insights. *Routledge Focus on Business and Management* presents small books on big topics and how they intersect with the world of business.

Individually, each title in the series provides coverage of a key academic topic, whilst collectively, the series forms a comprehensive collection across the business disciplines.

The Innovative Business School
Mentoring Today's Leaders for Tomorrow's Global Challenges
Edited by Daphne Halkias, Michael Neubert, Paul W. Thurman, Chris Adendorff and Sameh Abadir

Pop-Up Retail
The Evolution, Application and Future of Ephemeral Stores
Ghalia Boustani

Building Virtual Teams
Trust, Culture, and Remote Work
Catalina Dumitru

Fostering Wisdom at Work
Jeff M. Allen

Artificial Intelligence, Business and Civilization
Our Fate Made in Machines
Andreas Kaplan

For more information about this series, please visit: www.routledge.com/Routledge-Focus-on-Business-and-Management/book-series/FBM

Artificial Intelligence, Business and Civilization

Our Fate Made in Machines

Andreas Kaplan

Routledge
Taylor & Francis Group

LONDON AND NEW YORK

First published 2022
by Routledge
4 Park Square, Milton Park, Abingdon, Oxon OX14 4RN

and by Routledge
605 Third Avenue, New York, NY 10158

Routledge is an imprint of the Taylor & Francis Group, an informa business

British Library Cataloguing-in-Publication Data
A catalogue record for this book is available from the British Library

Library of Congress Cataloging-in-Publication Data
A catalog record for this book has been requested

ISBN: 978-1-032-15531-9 (hbk)
ISBN: 978-1-032-15533-3 (pbk)
ISBN: 978-1-003-24455-4 (ebk)

DOI: 10.4324/9781003244554

Typeset in Times New Roman
by Apex CoVantage, LLC

Contents

About the author

Andreas Kaplan's research focuses on decrypting the digital world, mainly artificial intelligence and social media. According to John Wiley & Sons, with a series of seminal publications and over 35,000 mentions on Google Scholar, Kaplan ranks among the top 50 business authors worldwide. Furthermore, a widely reported Stanford University study acknowledged Kaplan as one of the world's most-quoted and influential scientists. He is an internationally acclaimed author, keynote speaker, and advisor to governments and corporations.

Professor Kaplan engages especially in analyzing the future impact of advances in artificial intelligence on countries' economies and society at large. He asks questions about AI's opportunities as well as its risks. Much of his work addresses the necessity for regulation, education, a human approach to digitalization, and ethics regarding AI and its consequences for humanity. Kaplan is a founding member of the European Center for Digital Competitiveness.

Andreas M. Kaplan currently serves as Rector and Dean of ESCP Business School Paris, Sorbonne Alliance. He is executive education advisory board member of Kozminski University, Leadership Fellow at St. Georges House, Windsor Castle, as well as special advisor to the Institut Français de la Mode (IFM). Previously, Professor Kaplan served on the board of the German-French Economic Circle (DFWK), the academic council and steering committee of the Sorbonne Art et Métiers University, faculty member at ESSEC Business School, and senior lecturer at Sciences Po Paris.

Kaplan did his Habilitation at the Sorbonne (Université Paris 1 Panthéon-Sorbonne) and his PhD at the University of Cologne/HEC Paris. He holds a Master of Public Administration (MPA) from the École Nationale d'Administration (ENA; Class of République; Institut National du Service Public—ISP), an MSc from ESCP Business School, and a BSc from the University of Munich. Additionally, he was a visiting PhD student at INSEAD and participated in the International Teachers Program (ITP) at Kellogg School of Management, Northwestern University.

1 Commencements

AI, business, and civilization

The media regularly report on advances in artificial intelligence, such as AI-powered self-driving cars (Mills 2021) populating our roads in the near future, AI systems able to detect cancer at the same precision as the top medical experts (Svoboda 2020), as well as artificial intelligence and automation likely replacing many of our current jobs while at the same time creating new ones (Press 2019). Perhaps less known, to mention one example, is that most AI-driven voice assistants are equipped with a feminine tone, as female AI seems less intimidating, and studies show that all genders react more favorably to a female speaker (Borau 2021). Also, around two-thirds of those working in AI-related jobs being men might have triggered this choice. Even more intriguing might be Sophia, a female-appearing robot, who received citizenship of Saudi Arabia (Reynolds 2018). And in case you're less enthused about humanoids such as Sophia, you might appreciate knowing that by 2025, we will most likely have AI-driven pet robots that look, feel, and behave like actual animals.

Alongside these anecdotes is lots of press coverage of doomsday scenarios. Artificial intelligence might very well be the "worst event in the history of our civilization," as physicist Stephen Hawking declared at Web Summit in Lisbon (Kharpal 2017). Elon Musk, CEO of Tesla, also often warns about artificial intelligence, claiming that AI will overtake humans in less than five years and declaring it vastly more dangerous than North Korea (Gibbs 2017). Looking at examples such as a robot that noticed its decreased performance consequent to it losing both its mechanical legs, and which rebuilt itself by simple trial and error, not having been programmed to do so, is an eerie example of what Hawking or Musk have been telling us (Cully et al. 2015). Another spine-tingling example might be Stanford University scientists, who have developed an AI system able to predict the death of hospital patients with 90% accuracy (Johnson 2018). Moreover, imagining that intelligent machines take over thinking for us, some believe that humans will intellectually decline, with humans subsequently regressing to

DOI: 10.4324/9781003244554-1

more primitive forms. Just ask yourself if you could still find your way in an unknown city without Google Maps or correctly compose a memo without using spell check.

We've all come across these examples, dire predictions, and concerns. This book aims to provide nuance in this domain, clarifying what is fact and what is (still) dystopia. Moreover, it seeks to give a broad yet sound overview of AI in a concise and digestible format. To do so, Chapter 2 will define artificial intelligence, explain its various types, and briefly outline significant milestones in AI's past, present, and (likely or unlikely) future. This chapter will explain the confusion surrounding artificial intelligence and why AI, generally speaking, is challenging to grasp. Chapter 3 explains why AI is indeed a double-edged sword, and illustrates this with examples from higher education, from the workplace, and in governance and state. Chapter 4 analyses and decrypts how humanity might ensure AI's constructive use and utility for humans via regulation, ethical conduct, and wide-ranging AI literacy and education, as well as international cooperation. Chapter 5 consists of a series of case studies addressing Walmart, the strongly technophilic NYC Metropolitan Museum of Art, and China, "the planet's AI trAIning ground." The concluding remarks in Chapter 6 ruminate on whether human civilization's fate will be made in machines, as the title queries.

We can legitimately ask why AI has become such a buzzword, and why its advances affect both the workplace and beyond more strongly these last few years than the seven decades since AI's advent in the 1940s and 50s. First, we have seen a jump in (big) data availability due to digitalization, recently accentuated and accelerated by the Covid pandemic. In order to learn, AI systems need a huge quantity of data to improve and fine-tune the algorithms on which they run: The more data, the faster, higher performing, and precise a machine can become. Second, there has been an impressive increase in computational power at lower cost, enabling storing, processing, and analyzing the available data at a far greater scale and speed. Both these evolutions have rendered artificial intelligence not only a reality but also commercially viable. Therefore, many speak of the Fourth Industrial Revolution, while others consider the advances of artificial intelligence and its potential high importance, warranting an entirely new type of revolution on the level of the Agricultural Revolution having led to society, followed by the Industrial Revolution(s) having enhanced overall productivity, and now the AI Revolution, also called the Intelligence Revolution. While the Industrial Revolution augmented humans' mechanical strength, the Intelligence Revolution will drastically increase humans' intellectual power.

Regardless of whether AI progress falls within the Fourth Industrial Revolution or prompts its own intelligence era, it is clear that artificial intelligence will result in significant developments in all spheres. Google CEO Sundar Pichai paraphrased this evolution, stating that AI is one of the essential breakthroughs on which human civilization is currently working, which will be more life changing than our discovery of fire and electricity (Clifford 2018). Just thinking about how the latter two inventions transformed humanity gives us an idea of the impact that AI progress could have. To help you understand this impact, this book will give you insights, analyses, and food for thought. Essentially, it brings together reflections and ideas from recent works and builds on papers and articles co-written with colleagues, puts them in perspective, and adds real-life examples and case studies (for example Haenlein, Huang, and Kaplan 2021; Haenlein and Kaplan 2019, 2020; Haenlein et al. 2019; Kaplan 2020a, 2020b, 2020c, 2020d, 2020e, 2020f, 2020g, 2021a, 2021b, 2021c; Kaplan and Haenlein 2019a, 2019b; Kaplan and Haenlein 2020; Libai et al. 2020; Malagocka, Mazurek, and Kaplan 2022; Pucciarelli and Kaplan 2022). Accordingly, this book is of interest to anybody seeking to understand AI in its broad scope and discover its promises and the concerns that it elicits; what is already feasible; and what our future might look like.

References

Borau, Sylvie (2021) Female Robots Are Seen as Being the Most Human: Why?, *The Conversation*, April 16.
Clifford, Catherine (2018) Google CEO: AI Is More Important Than Fire or Electricity, *CNBC*, February 1.
Cully, Antoine, Clune Jeff, Tarapore Danesh, Mouret Jean-Baptiste (2015) Robots That Can Adapt Like Animals, *Nature*, 521, 503–507.
Gibbs, Samuel (2017) Elon Musk: AI 'Vastly More Risky Than North Korea', *The Guardian*, August 14.
Haenlein, Michael, Huang Ming-Hui, Kaplan Andreas (2021) Business Ethics in the Era of Artificial Intelligence, *Journal of Business Ethics*.
Haenlein, Michael, Kaplan Andreas (2019) A Brief History of AI: On the Past, Present, and Future of Artificial Intelligence, *California Management Review*, 61(4), 5–14.
Haenlein, Michael, Kaplan Andreas (2020) Artificial Intelligence and Robotics: Shaking Up the Business World and Society at Large, *Journal of Business Research*, 124, 405–407.
Haenlein, Michael, Kaplan Andreas, Tan Chee-Wee, Zhang Pengzhu (2019) Artificial Intelligence (AI) and Management Analytics, *Journal of Management Analytics*, 6(4), 341–343.
Johnson, Lloyd (2018) Scientists Use AI to Predict When You Will Die: With 90% Accuracy, *Express*, January 19.
Kaplan, Andreas (2020a) Artificial Intelligence, Social Media, and Fake News: Is This the End of Democracy?, in Gül, A. A., Ertürk, Y. D. and Elmer, P. (eds.),

Digital Transformation in Media and Society. Istanbul, Turkey: Istanbul University Press Books, 149–161.

Kaplan, Andreas (2020b) Artificial Intelligence, Marketing, and the Fourth Industrial Revolution: Clarifications, Challenges, Concerns, in Christiansen, B. and Škrinjarić, T. (eds.), *Handbook of Research on Applied AI for International Business and Marketing Applications*. Hershey, Pennsylvania: IGI, 1–13.

Kaplan, Andreas (2020c) Artificial Intelligence: Emphasis on Ethics & Education, *International Journal of Swarm Intelligence and Evolutionary Computation*, 9(3).

Kaplan, Andreas (2020d) Hochschulbildung in Zeiten der Künstlichen Intelligenz, in Nachtwei, J. and Sureth, A. (eds.), *Sonderband Zukunft der Arbeit*, Band 12, Berlin: Human Resources Consulting Review, 153–156.

Kaplan, Andreas (2020e) Retailing and the Ethical Challenges and Dilemmas Behind Artificial Intelligence, in Eleonora, P. (ed.), *Retail Futures: The Good, the Bad and the Ugly of the Digital Transformation*. Bingley, UK: Emerald Publishing, 181–191.

Kaplan, Andreas (2020f) Social Media Powered by Artificial Intelligence, Violence and Nonviolence, in Kurtz, L. (ed.), *Encyclopedia of Violence, Peace & Conflict* (3rd ed.). Cambridge, MA: Elsevier.

Kaplan, Andreas (2020g) Marrying Cultural Heritage and High Tech: The Use of ARTificial Intelligence in Museums (Beijing's Palace Museum, NYC's Met, and Paris' Louvre), The Case Centre, Case 320–0057–1.

Kaplan, Andreas (2021a) Artificial Intelligence (AI): When Humans and Machines Might Have to Coexist, in Verdegem, P. (ed.), *AI for Everyone? Critical Perspectives*. London: University of Westminster Press, 21–32.

Kaplan, Andreas (2021b) *Higher Education at the Crossroads of Disruption: The University of the 21st Century, Great Debates in Higher Education*. Bingley, UK: Emerald Publishing.

Kaplan, Andreas (2021c) Your Attention, Please: You've Got 15 Seconds! TikTok and How Organizations Can Make Use of It, in Kolukirik, S. (ed.), *Digitalization and Future of Digital Society*. Berlin, Germany: Peter Lang Publishing House, 367–378.

Kaplan, Andreas, Haenlein Michael (2019a) Digital Transformation and Disruption, On Big Data, Blockchain, Artificial Intelligence, and Other Things, *Business Horizons*, 62(6), 679–681.

Kaplan, Andreas, Haenlein Michael (2019b) Siri, Siri in My Hand, Who Is the Fairest in the Land? On the Interpretations, Illustrations and Implications of Artificial Intelligence, *Business Horizons*, 62(1), 15–25.

Kaplan, Andreas, Haenlein Michael (2020) Rulers of the World, Unite! The Challenges and Opportunities of Artificial Intelligence, *Business Horizons*, 63(1), 37–50.

Kharpal, Arjun (2017) Stephen Hawking Says AI Could Be 'Worst Event in the History of Our Civilization', *CNBC*, November 6.

Libai, Barak, Bart Yakov, Gensler Sonja, Hofacker Charles, Kaplan Andreas, Köttenheinrich Kim, Kroll Eike (2020) A Brave New World? On AI and the Management of Customer Relationships, *Journal of Interactive Marketing*, 51(C), 44–56.

Malagocka, Karolina, Mazurek Grzegorz, Kaplan Andreas (2022) Virtual Worlds, Virtual Reality, and Augmented Reality: Review, Synthesis and Research

Agenda, in Yan, Z. (ed.), *Cambridge Handbook of Cyber Behavior*. Cambridge: Cambridge University Press.

Mills, Terrence (2021) Artificial Intelligence: Where It Is Working and Where It Is Not, *Forbes*, May 24.

Press, Gil (2019) Is AI Going to Be a Jobs Killer? New Reports about the Future of Work, *Forbes*, July 15.

Pucciarelli, Francesca, Kaplan Andreas (2022) Voice-Powered Artificial Intelligence: Opportunities, Challenges and Marketing Implications of Voice Assistants, in Yan, Z. (ed.), *Cambridge Handbook of Cyber Behavior*. Cambridge: Cambridge University Press.

Reynolds, Emily (2018) The Agony of Sophia, the World's First Robot Citizen Condemned to a Lifeless Career in Marketing, *Wired*, June 1.

Svoboda, Elizabeth (2020) Artificial Intelligence Is Improving the Detection of Lung Cancer, *Nature*, November 18.

2 Clarifications
AI, big data, the internet-of-things, and robotics

Several misconceptions exist surrounding the term "artificial intelligence." To clarify what AI is, one needs first to understand why such confusion prevails. For our purposes, we define artificial intelligence as "a system's ability to interpret external data correctly, to learn from such data, and to use those learnings to achieve specific goals and tasks through flexible adaptation" (Kaplan and Haenlein 2019, p. 17). Based on this by-now broadly applied definition in both theory and practice, we will compare AI to related terms, notably big data, the internet-of-things (IoT), machine learning, deep learning, and robotics. Moreover, a taxonomy of various artificial intelligence types will be presented, categorizing AI into analytical, human-inspired, and humanized artificial intelligence. Airbnb will serve as an example to illustrate these various AI types. Finally, AI's history and evolution will be briefly surveyed, beginning with the AI spring (AI's birth), followed by a couple of AI summers and winters (ups and downs in AI funding and science), and concluding in AI's current fall period, or harvest of the fruits of past AI research and development.

a. What is (and is not) artificial intelligence?

What exactly is artificial intelligence? A search for the term can lead to exasperation and confusion. Results of such an online quest will provide several definitions and notions of AI. Therefore, it is essential to first explain why there is so much ambiguity before arriving at a definition for it, and to subsequently distinguish AI from similar yet not identical concepts. There are at least five reasons why it is not straightforward to describe artificial intelligence (Kaplan and Haenlein 2020):

1   First of all, fiction provides us with an incorrect or distorted image of AI, especially Hollywood blockbusters such as *The Matrix* or *The Terminator*. Also, the media repeatedly report on AI somewhat sensationally, focusing on doomsday and apocalyptic scenarios to generate

DOI: 10.4324/9781003244554-2

higher ratings and increase clicks. As early as the 1940s, when the first general-purpose computer was launched, headlines described it as "mathematical Frankenstein." Such media coverage leads to incorrect ideas of what AI is and is not, a phenomenon that Carnegie Mellon's Zachary Lipton calls the "artificial intelligence misinformation epidemic" (Schwartz 2018).

2 Misconceptions about AI can be explained by the so-called AI effect (Haenlein and Kaplan 2019, 2020): While we might have considered something to be artificial intelligence in the past, as soon as we get used to machines performing a given task, we consequently no longer think of it as artificial intelligence. To a certain extent, due to this effect, a definition for AI is a moving target, giving the impression that it must be something that is constantly out of reach and lies in the future. This is similar to Gartner's hype cycle, which explains that innovations such as self-driving cars follow a typical path in consumer response, from overenthusiasm through disillusionment to an eventual comprehension of the emerging technology's actual capability.

3 As we know, defining human intelligence is not an easy endeavor, and accordingly, applying such a concept to machines is at least of equal complexity. Howard Gardner (1999, pp. 33–34), for example, defines intelligence as "biopsychological potential to process information . . . to solve problems or create products that are of value in a culture." Gardner's is only one of many definitions of intelligence. Scientists, however, usually do not define human intelligence according to only one parameter, but rather as per a combination of several distinct abilities, rendering its application to its artificial version even more difficult.

4 AI appears in a variety of versions and can be categorized into various forms (cf. Section 2b), depending upon a given system's cognitive, emotional, and social competencies, which can easily be conflated. Differing types of AI, all exhibiting differing capabilities, result in further uncertainty regarding defining artificial intelligence. Moreover, AI has three evolutionary phases (cf. Section 2c): artificial narrow intelligence, artificial general intelligence, and artificial superintelligence, which also complicates arriving at a definition of what artificial intelligence is (Kaplan and Haenlein 2019).

5 Finally, big data, the internet-of-things, machine and deep learning, as well as robotics, while related to artificial intelligence, do not denote the same idea, leading to additional confusion and potential for misconceptions.

The term "artificial intelligence" is said to have been coined during the Dartmouth Research Project, a conference in the summer of 1956 that convened an interdisciplinary group of researchers and scientists. When proposing this workshop and inviting attendees one year in advance, John McCarthy, Marvin Minsky, Nathaniel Rochester, and Claude Shannon, often considered AI's founding fathers, characterized AI as "making a machine behave in ways that would be called intelligent if a human were so behaving" (McCarthy et al. 1955). Minsky later defined it as "the science of making machines do things that would require intelligence if done by men" (Minsky 1968, p. v). John McCarthy (2007) provided an expanded definition in his revised 2007 paper, describing AI as "the science and engineering of making intelligent machines, especially intelligent computer programs." For our purposes, focusing particularly on how AI imitates human intelligence, artificial intelligence is described and defined as "a system's ability to interpret external data correctly, to learn from such data, and to use those learnings to achieve specific goals and tasks through flexible adaptation" (Kaplan and Haenlein 2019, p. 17).

A multitude of further descriptions and definitions can be found, some of which are as follows: Huang and Rust (2018) described AI as "machines that exhibit aspects of human intelligence"; Longoni, Bonezzi, and Morewedge (2019) wrote of "Algorithms to perform perceptual, cognitive, and conversational functions of the human mind"; Davenport et al. (2020) cited "Programs, algorithms, systems, and machines that demonstrate intelligence"; Ma and Sun (2020) cited "Machine behavior that would be called intelligent if a human was behaving in the same way"; and Puntoni et al. (2021) talk about "an ecosystem that performs tasks requiring intelligence and autonomous decision making." Finally, colleagues together with Praveen Kopalle (2022), also a Dartmouth professor, define artificial intelligence as "programs, algorithms, systems, and machines that mimic intelligent human behavior." This list shows that even the scientific community is confounded at consistently defining the concept of artificial intelligence, not to mention layfolk's understanding of it.

So why are we so intent on defining AI? Because doing so enables its distinction from similar concepts and explaining how these relate to and differ from artificial intelligence. "The internet-of-things" (Krotov 2017; Saarikko, Westergren, and Blomquist 2017), for example, expresses the notion that "devices around us are equipped with sensors and software to collect and exchange data" (Kaplan and Haenlein 2019, p. 17). IoT relates to AI as one way of collecting the external data nodes constituting an entryway for artificial intelligence. Consequently, the internet-of-things provides a source of big data, summarized by Kaplan and Haenlein (2019, p. 17) as "data sets characterized by huge quantities (volume) of frequently updated data (velocity) in various formats, such as numeric, textual, or images/videos (variety)." Further means to collecting big data can be an organization's internal databases or (mobile) social media (Kaplan 2012; Kaplan and Haenlein 2010). Machine learning, then, is applied to identify the explanatory mechanism, patterns, and rules in these (big) data sets, and it summarizes methods that enable AI systems to learn without having explicitly been programmed for such respective learning outcomes. Therefore, machine learning is a fundamental element of artificial intelligence, yet constitutes only one part thereof, as AI also has the capacity to sense data via image and voice recognition or, for example, natural language processing. "Deep learning," often incorrectly used interchangeably with "machine learning," is a subfield of the latter and based on neural networks, that is, computing systems that imitate biological neural networks that comprise the human brain. Finally, robotics combines engineering and computer science and encompasses the design, development, operation, and application of physical robots. Combined with artificial intelligence, robotics may lead to human-like robots, such as the aforementioned Sophia, that mimic human behavior, thinking, and intelligence. At the moment, however, most robots are not artificially intelligent and, on the contrary, typically perform at limited functionality.

All this is to say that there are nearly as many different definitions of artificial intelligence as there are experts and scientists who work therein. This multiplicity has several implications, such as difficulty codifying a clear legal framework regulating artificial intelligence on a global scale—as different legislators assign (slightly) differing contours to AI, potentially leading to differing regulations depending upon locale. While this situation per se exists in many domains, in the case of artificial intelligence, there are a few specificities to be considered that will be addressed in Chapter 4. Perhaps the most straightforward AI definition is provided by Wikipedia (Kaplan and Haenlein 2014), where it is simply defined as "intelligence demonstrated by machines."

b. Classifying, exemplifying, and envisioning

We base our classification of various AI systems on the vast competencies literature dividing intelligence into three types (Kaplan and Haenlein 2019):

1   Analytical AI: This type of artificial intelligence exhibits parameters consistent with cognition only (i.e., faculties linked to systematic reasoning and pattern recognition) and develops a mental representation of a particular phenomenon via the help of previous experience. Today's AI applications are essentially analytical, with voice or image recognition as prominent examples.
2   Human-inspired AI: This type of artificial intelligence additionally exhibits parameters of emotional intelligence (for example adaptability,

achievement orientation, emotional self-awareness, self-confidence); that is, it can detect and understand human emotions and take them into account for its tasks and goals. AI systems cannot (yet) experience emotions themselves, but they can identify them through, for example, the assessment of facial expressions or changes in voice.

3   Humanized AI: Finally, this type of artificial intelligence exhibits cognitive, emotional, and social parameters (for example teamwork, charisma, empathy). Not yet existent, humanized AI systems would have to be self-aware and self-conscious in their interplay with humans to fall into this category. For the moment, such systems are more a case of fantasizing about the future than reality.

In addition, phenomena that are referred to as AI, strictly speaking, do not belong to any of the prior categories, adding to the confusion and misconceptions surrounding artificial intelligence. For example, IBM's often-cited chess-playing algorithm, Deep Blue, which beat chess grandmaster Garry Kasparov at the end of the 1990s, was not artificial intelligence according to the aforementioned definition, but rather an "expert system." What is the difference? Expert systems are based on a multitude of rules in the form of if/then statements. These rules are designed by humans and programmed into the expert system, which cannot autonomously learn from external data, as the rules are preconfigured. Actual AI derives rules on its own by analyzing vast quantities of (big) data, and is therefore capable of autonomous learning.

Expert systems and AI systems pursue two utterly differing approaches in their attempt to mimic human intelligence. Expert systems apply a top-down procedure (also characterized as knowledge-based or symbolic approach) wherein human intelligence is codified and reconstructed in so many rules. AI systems, in contrast, apply a bottom-up mechanism (also termed as behavior-based or connectionist approach) using (big) data to formulate "rules" autonomously through neural networks and deep learning. As an example, let's look at how each system would detect an elephant: An expert system first would have to be programmed by a human with a set of rules allowing identifying an elephant (for example four legs, a trunk, a tale, a specific size and coloring). We can immediately see the complexity of formulating such rules that permit the system to differentiate between an elephant and, for example, a rhinoceros. AI systems, on the other hand, do not necessitate such pre-codification, but rather formulate their own rules by analyzing thousands of elephant images, enabling them to describe and detect an elephant in their own "language." Therefore, a bottom-up approach enables far more complex tasks and goals than expert systems could handle.

To illustrate AI using the example of an actual company, let's look at Airbnb, the online platform for offering and finding lodging. Airbnb strongly applies AI in its various actions, especially for its service development, dynamic pricing, and the detection and reduction of discriminatory behavior. Before Airbnb began using analytical AI, it used decision trees to program a variety of expert systems previously in place. This approach enabled relatively low calibration of search outcomes and subsequent lists of lodging options. However, analytical AI was a game-changer, enabling Airbnb to provide totally personalized offerings and customized solutions (Kaplan 2006; Kaplan and Haenlein 2006; Kaplan, Schoder, and Haenlein 2007; Schoder et al. 2006).

To provide users with the optimal list of available lodgings, Airbnb's analytical AI considers several parameters: What locales is the guest looking for? How much time does s/he spend looking at them, that is, stay on the respective webpage? How much did they pay for their recent stays? What ratings have they given their past stays? Mike Curtis, vice president of engineering at Airbnb, explained that the platform's objective is to offer the best possible service and experience to the guest, and that this is feasible as "We don't just want to get a booking for the sake of a booking; we want you to book something that is a great experience" (Heathman 2018). Additionally, AI also purports to know better than customers do what the latter want and suggests recommendations that would not otherwise be part of the searcher's consideration set. Moreover, not only are guests given an optimized listing of suggestions for lodgings, but also hosts are provided with an optimized pricing proposal. Tourism being a highly seasonal sector, with specific locales asking wildly differing prices depending upon the time of year, Airbnb uses AI-driven dynamic pricing, adapting its suggestions for prices daily and instantly adjusting them to constantly changing conditions. The probability of booking, prices in the accommodation's surroundings, lodgings' previous reviews in both quality and quantity, and the weather forecast for the area are only some of the AI system analyses' elements for formulating its pricing suggestions.

AI is used not only for direct business, but also to identify and reduce discrimination. A study conducted by Edelman, Luca, and Svirsky (2017) showed that in contrast to users with Caucasian-sounding names, those whose names sounded like African-American users were 16% less likely to be given the lodging they wanted. Consequently, Airbnb began a series of anti-discrimination measures: Hosts were asked to sign an agreement to provide accommodations independently of searchers' (perceived) origins. If a host denies a particular booking, the system automatically assumes that the listing is not available during the respective dates and consequently blocks it to all searchers for that period. If the host nonetheless wishes to rent out the lodging for those dates, s/he needs to manually unblock those dates in the system. Additionally, s/he must respond to queries regarding the reasons for having denied the initial booking to a certain user. All of these measures are supported by analytical artificial intelligence working in the background.

Moving from analytical to human-inspired AI could bring the platform to the next level. For example, Airbnb could identify a potential guest's emotions via facial expression analyses when looking at the various listings' images and videos. This information could then be used to fine-tune future suggestions. One might even imagine guests scrolling through the offerings together if traveling in a group: The AI system detects each group member's emotions, suggesting the best compromise to lead to the best cumulative satisfaction of the group. Humanized AI, finally, could simply keep you company during your entire vacation and talk to you when you seek some company, or remain silent if not. Moreover, it might decrypt the exchanges among the various group members, their emotions, and their social interactions, and accordingly adapt suggestions for day trips or various other activities. For example, if the AI system should detect tension, it might suggest splitting up the group, offering them various activities; or if it should detect fatigue, it might suggest some downtime at the beach; or in case of boredom, a visit to a theme park, escape room, or live entertainment.

Such fantasizing about what humanized AI might look like quickly leads to the question of whether there are/will be things that AI cannot do and which remain exclusively in the purview of human beings. This question is difficult to answer, as bottom line, nobody can see into the future. While creativity in the sense of how Albert Einstein described it as "intelligence having fun" might be such a domain, here too examples exist that call into doubt such ability. For example, Botnik Studios, an entertainment company, created an AI system that autonomously learned the writing style of Harry Potter novels by reading and analyzing all seven of them. The result was the machine writing a three-pager titled "Harry Potter and the Portrait of What Looked Like a Large Pile of Ash" (Beck 2017).

c. AI's past, present, and (future) perspective

While it is undoubtedly tricky to pinpoint the exact beginning of AI's history (Haenlein and Kaplan 2019), Alan Turing's (1950) paper "Computing Machinery and Intelligence" is often considered AI's scientific debut. However, the term "artificial intelligence" was not yet in use. Before that period, computers lacked memory capacity and could only execute commands but not store them, which is a prerequisite for AI to work. Therefore, in his seminal article, Turing asked, "Can machines think?" and described the now widely known Turing Test. This test is supposed to identify a system's capacity to show intelligence identical to and indistinguishable from that of a human. The evaluator, a human being conscious that one of the conversation partners is a computer, tries to detect if s/he is corresponding in writing with a human or a machine. If the assessor is unable to differentiate, then the AI-driven system passes the Turing Test; that is, the machine is said to exhibit (artificial) intelligence (Turing 1950).

Alongside Turing's research, we also need to cite a well-known work of fiction that is often raised as having been highly influential in artificial intelligence's first steps. In 1942, science fiction novelist Isaac Asimov wrote his short story "Runaround" published in the 1950 *I, Robot* collection, telling of the adventures of engineers Mike Donavan and Gregory Powell, who developed a robot. Part of this story are the Three Robotics Laws: (1) A robot must not endanger a human being or, via inertia, enable a human to get hurt; (2) A robot must follow a human being's orders unless obedience would go against the aforementioned first law; and (3) An AI-powered robot must assure its survival unless such action would conflict with the first two laws. Interestingly, these once-fictional laws currently form the basis for reflections on legal questions and policy discussions on how humans should use robots, algorithms, and AI systems. Thus, Asimov's story doubtlessly spurred thousands of scientists from then until today to dedicate themselves to advancing artificial intelligence.

Four such inspired researchers were AI's aforementioned founding fathers, who upon organizing the Dartmouth Summer Research Project on Artificial Intelligence (DSRPAI), kicked off AI's spring season. As aforementioned, it was during this conference that the term "AI" was coined, and therefore it can be considered AI's official birth. The eight-week-long workshop aimed at bringing together scientists from a broad variety of domains to launch a new field of research: developing machines able to mimic human intelligence. Workshop attendees would become the leaders in AI progress on a global scale (Russel and Norvig 2019), prompting research in the field of artificial intelligence for the next two decades.

Following AI's spring was a series of AI summers and winters, a metaphor for the highs and lows of AI research and its funding. Two success stories triggered the euphoria in the wake of the first AI summer, resulting in a multitude of AI research projects. The first one was MIT professor Joseph Weizenbaum's creation of the ELIZA computer program, a natural language processing software capable of mimicking a conversation with an actual human being. ELIZA was also one of the first attempts to pass the Turing Test. The second is Nobel Prize laureate for economics Herbert Simon, who, together with his colleagues, invented the General Problem Solver program to tackle simple tasks and games such as the Tower of

Hanoi, a mathematical puzzle consisting of three rods and a number of disks of various sizes that can be dropped onto any rod. Beginning with the disks piled on the first rod from biggest to smallest, the game is solved when the entire pile is moved from the first to the third rod while obeying two rules: (1) Only one disk at a time may be moved, a move being taking the top disk from one pile and putting it either on an empty rod or on top of another pile; (2) A disk may only be placed on top of a bigger one (Colman 2008).

While solving the Tower of Hanoi would nowadays hardly be identified as particularly intelligent, when it was invented, it was a sensation. Optimism thereabout grew into an over-hyped bubble that peaked in the early 1970s when Minsky predicted in an interview with *Life* magazine that systems exhibiting an average human's intelligence would exist in as few as three and a maximum of eight years from then (Darrach 1970). Soon after this interview, it became apparent that the entire AI community had grossly underestimated the difficulty of AI's development: At the time, little information could be stored on computers, and they were too weak and slow to exhibit more advanced intelligent behavior. Subsequently, the first AI winter began with severe budget cuts for AI research, supported by the US Congress roundly criticizing high spending on AI research, and the British Science Research Council publishing a strongly negative report on AI's progress in 1973, prompting challenging times for the AI community (Haenlein and Kaplan 2019).

A second "AI summer" began in the 1980s, when Japan began to invest heavily in decrypting artificial intelligence, shortly followed by the US and other governments "rediscovering" AI research and providing billions of dollars in funding. Edward Feigenbaum introduced the aforementioned expert systems, which subsequently became widely used in industry. Moreover, David Rumelhart and John Hopfield promoted machine and deep learning, enabling systems to learn from past events. Yet neither did this second AI summer lead to anticipated results; it was followed by a second period of low funding, or "winter," in the late 1980s/early 1990s, with disillusioned investors again withdrawing their funding. Nonetheless, despite budget reductions, AI research would advance during this period. On May 11, 1997, Deep Blue became the first chess computer to beat world champion Garry Kasparov. The supercomputer could handle double the number of moves per second than was the case for its first match (which Deep Blue lost). Deep Blue's win was broadcast live, with over 70 million viewers and high press coverage, prompting a resurgence of interest in artificial intelligence, even though as aforementioned, Deep Blue is strictly speaking an expert system and does not fall into the category of actual artificial intelligence (Newborn 2002).

During the 2010s, new hype began developing around AI, mainly for two reasons. First, enhanced access to big data: To be able to train algorithms, you need millions of data points, or big data. Second, computational power to accelerate the calculation of learning algorithms had massively improved. Thus, a complete paradigm shift away from expert systems and toward AI systems took place: It was no longer necessary to program rules for expert systems, but instead computers can learn rules autonomously by correlation and classification, based on massive datasets. AI's fall—or the harvest of the fruits of past research—is considered to have officially begun in 2015 with the development of Google's AlphaGo program, which applied deep learning and neural networks, enabling it to face the world Go (a highly complex game) champion and win. Go's complexity is of such amplitude that it was previously believed that machines could never beat humans (Metz 2016).

Currently, we are only at the beginning of this new era and AI's fall season. All artificial intelligence in use currently falls into the first generation of AI systems, also termed "artificial narrow intelligence" (ANI), or weak, below-human-level AI (Kaplan and Haenlein 2019). While these first-generation systems usually outperform or equal human beings in the specific area for which they are programmed, they are not considered to be generally intelligent (therefore characterized as "below-human-level AI"). These applications perform a particular task only and cannot autonomously solve problems in other domains. A self-driving car, for example, can take you from Location A to Location B, but it would not be able to autonomously learn how to provide first aid in the case of a collision (although it is most likely programmed to automatically dial emergency services and give them the accident's exact location).

In the future, artificial general intelligence (AGI), AI's second generation, also called "strong, human-level AI," might plan, think, and work out solutions on its own for problems and activities for which it has not been programmed at its origins. Such systems would equal and outperform human beings in many domains. The aforementioned self-driving car is a classic example, autonomously learning how to assist injured passengers after a collision. In this situation, the AI system would probably no longer be a car, but rather a human-like robot-driven unit. AI's second generation thus comes pretty close to the robots we've seen in Hollywood blockbusters.

At some point in humanity's future, we might even attain AI's third and ultimate generation, artificial superintelligence (ASI), or conscious/self-aware, surpassing-human-level AI. In this currently very futuristic scenario, machines would be genuinely self-aware, apply AI to any area, consistently outperform humans, and problem solve any domain instantaneously. For example, in such a world of artificial superintelligence, the human-like robot driving any car would detect when its passengers would like to engage in conversation and when they prefer a silent environment. Moreover, such robots would metamorphize into first aid providers if need be, retrieve your groceries and carry them into your home, or occupy your children (and keep them safe) while you leave the car to get cash from an ATM—or better yet, they would get cash for you.

References

Asimov, Isaac (1950) Runaround, in Asimov, I. and Regn, J. (eds.) Robot, I. (The Isaac Asimov Collection). New York City: Doubleday, 40.

Beck, Kellen (2017) A Hilarious New Harry Potter Chapter Was Written by a Predictive Keyboard: And It's Perfect, *Mashable.com*, December 12.

Colman, Andrew M. (2008) *A Dictionary of Psychology* (3rd ed.). Oxford: Oxford University Press.

Darrach, Brad (1970) Meet Shakey, the First Electronic Person, *Life*, November 20, 58–68.

Davenport, Thomas, Guha Abhijit, Grewal Dhruv, Bressgott Timna (2020) How Artificial Intelligence will Change the Future of Marketing, *Journal of the Academy of Marketing Science*, 48, 24–42.

Edelman, Benjamin, Luca Michael, Svirsky Dan (2017) Racial Discrimination in the Sharing Economy: Evidence from a Field Experiment, *American Economic Journal: Applied Economics*, 9(2), 1–22.

Gardner, Howard (1999) *Intelligence Reframed: Multiple Intelligences for the 21st Century*. New York: Basic Books.

Haenlein, Michael, Kaplan Andreas (2019) A Brief History of AI: On the Past, Present, and Future of Artificial Intelligence, *California Management Review*, 61(4), 5–14.

Haenlein, Michael, Kaplan Andreas (2020) Artificial Intelligence and Robotics: Shaking Up the Business World and Society at Large, *Journal of Business Research*, 124, 405–407.

Heathman, Amelia (2018) How AI Is Powering Airbnb's Mission to Change How We Travel Forever, *Evening Standard*, April 17.

Huang, Ming-Hui, Rust Roland (2018) Artificial Intelligence in Service, *Journal of Service Research*, 21(2), 155–172.

Kaplan, Andreas (2006) Factors Influencing the Adoption of Mass Customization: Determinants, Moderating Variables and Cross-National Generalizability, Cuvillier, Goettingen.

Kaplan, Andreas (2012) If You Love Something, Let It Go Mobile: Mobile Marketing and Mobile Social Media 4×4, *Business Horizons*, 55(2), 129–139.

Kaplan, Andreas, Haenlein Michael (2006) Toward a Parsimonious Definition of Traditional and Electronic Mass Customization, *Journal of Product Innovation Management*, 23(2), 168–182.

Kaplan, Andreas, Haenlein Michael (2010) Users of the World, Unite! The Challenges and Opportunities of Social Media, *Business Horizons*, 53(1), 59–68.

Kaplan, Andreas, Haenlein Michael (2014) Collaborative Projects (Social Media Application): About Wikipedia, the Free Encyclopedia, *Business Horizons*, 57(5), 617–626.

Kaplan, Andreas, Haenlein Michael (2019) Siri, Siri in My Hand, Who Is the Fairest in the Land? On the Interpretations, Illustrations and Implications of Artificial Intelligence, *Business Horizons*, 62(1), 15–25.

Kaplan, Andreas, Haenlein Michael (2020) Rulers of the World, Unite! The Challenges and Opportunities of Artificial Intelligence, *Business Horizons*, 63(1), 37–50.

Kaplan, Andreas, Schoder Detlef, Haenlein Michael (2007) Factors Influencing the Adoption of Mass Customization: The Impact of Base Category Consumption Frequency and Need Satisfaction, *Journal of Product Innovation Management*, 24(2), 101–116.

Kopalle, Praveen, Gangwar Manish, Kaplan Andreas, Ramachandran Divya, Reinartz Werner, Rindfleisch Aric (2022) Examining Artificial Intelligence (AI) Technologies in Marketing Via a Global Lens: Current Trends and Future Research Opportunities, *International Journal of Research in Marketing*, forthcoming.

Krotov, Vlad (2017) The Internet of Things and New Business Opportunities, *Business Horizons*, 60(6), 831–841.

Longoni, Chiara, Bonezzi Andrea, Morewedge Carey K. (2019) Resistance to Medical Artificial Intelligence, *Journal of Consumer Research*, 46(4), 629–650.

Ma, Liye, Baohong Sun (2020) Machine Learning and AI in Marketing: Connecting Computer Power to Human Insights, *International Journal of Research in Marketing*, 37(3), 481–504.

McCarthy, John (2007) What Is Artificial Intelligence?, Computer Science Department, Stanford University.

McCarthy, John, Minsky Marvin L., Rochester Nathaniel, Shannon Claude E. (1955) *A Proposal for the Dartmouth Summer Research Project on Artificial Intelligence*. Available at www-formal.stanford.edu/jmc/history/dartmouth/dartmouth.html.

Metz, Cade (2016) What the AI Behind AlphaGo Can Teach Us about Being Human, *Wired*, May 19.

Minsky, Marvin L. (1968) *Semantic Information Processing*. Cambridge: MIT Press.

Newborn, Monty (2002) *Deep Blue: An Artificial Intelligence Milestone*. New York, US: Springer.

Puntoni, Stefano, Walker Reczek Rebecca, Giesler Markus, Botti Simona (2021) Consumer and Artificial Intelligence: An Experiential Perspective, *Journal of Marketing*, 85, 131–151.

Russel, Stuart, Norvig Peter (2019) *Artificial Intelligence: A Modern Approach* (4th ed.) Hoboken, New Jersey.

Saarikko, Ted, Westergren Ulrika H., Blomquist Tomas (2017) The Internet of Things: Are Uou Ready for What's Coming?, *Business Horizons*, 60(5), 667–676.

Schoder, Detlef, Sick Stefan, Putzke Johannes, Kaplan Andreas (2006) Mass Customization in the Newspaper Industry: Consumers' Attitudes toward Individualized Media Innovations, *International Journal on Media Management*, 8(1), 9–18.

Schwartz, Oscar (2018) 'The Discourse Is Unhinged': How the Media Gets AI Alarmingly Wrong, *The Guardian*, July 25.

Turing, Alan (1950) Computing Machinery and Intelligence, *Mind*, 59(236), 433–460.

3 Concerns

AI's double-edged sword in education, enterprises, and elections

Artificial intelligence embodies both opportunities and threats. Like any technology, depending upon the human using it, AI can be applied for good or for bad. For example, AI can defend against cyberattacks or commit them. This chapter will shed light on AI's double-edged character both in the workplace and regarding democracy and the general manipulation of opinions. However, we'll begin our analysis with the educational sector, where much of AI's progress originated. Higher education has already begun to be transformed by artificial intelligence, which enables, for example, a customized and adapted approach based on learning analytics, that is, the big data of the educational sector. Looking into the future, we might ask if human educators might be replaced by machines altogether. Within companies, AI has and will have a substantial impact as well: It's no longer news that jobs will disappear due to AI, while new ones, many of which are as yet unknown, will be created. Finally, artificial intelligence could become a threat to democracy, particularly when combined with social media such as TikTok (Kaplan 2021c), Twitter (Kaplan and Haenlein 2011), and Foursquare (Kaplan 2012).

a. Did higher education dig its own grave by developing AI?

Much of the essential progress in AI originated in academia (Kaplan and Haenlein 2019). As aforementioned, the term "artificial intelligence" was coined at a seminar held at Dartmouth College, broadly launching AI as a research domain (Haenlein and Kaplan 2019). Also, the aforementioned victory of AlphaGo over the world champion Go player took place in academia: Two of the masterminds behind AlphaGo had been colleagues in University College London's Gatsby Computational Neuroscience Unit before launching DeepMind, AlphaGo's parent company, later acquired by Google. Several additional examples exist of artificial intelligence's milestones occurring in academia. For several years now, higher education has

DOI: 10.4324/9781003244554-3

been increasingly affected by AI, opening up many possibilities for the sector. However, if AI's evolution continues, we might legitimately ask whether higher education is digging its own grave, at least in the sector as we know it, by embracing artificial intelligence (Kaplan 2021a, 2022).

Jill Watson, a name inspired by IBM's Watson, is undoubtedly the most prominent example of an AI system in a university. Designed by Ashok K. Goel, professor in Interactive Computing at the Georgia Institute of Technology, Jill Watson is an artificially intelligent chatbot acting as a teaching assistant. Now used in several courses and programs, Jill began her career in the Knowledge-Based Artificial Intelligence (Computer Science 7637) course in Georgia Tech's OMSCS (Online Master of Science in Computer Science) program (Kaplan 2021b). The course enrolled 300 students, who posted more than 10,000 messages and queries per semester to an online message board, many of which were similar in nature. Thus, developing an AI-driven teaching assistant helping the human TAs cope with this ever-increasing volume. With his team, Professor Goel trained Jill on historical data before "letting her loose" on the message board in 2016. Since then, Jill has a 97% success rate responding to student inquiries. Responses were of such quality that many of the students did not realize that they were communicating with a machine. By answering approximately 40% of the queries, Jill freed up significant time for her human counterparts, who could consequently focus on higher-value work such as assisting students with their coursework, motivating them to study, and encouraging them in their progress (Leopold 2017; McFarland 2016).

Even before students begin a program, AI can significantly help universities, which increasingly apply AI during the recruitment process. Element451, an AI-powered customer relationship management (CRM) system used for student enrollment, analyzes applications by, for example, looking at an applicants' interactions with the university's website, their demographics, transcript, and so forth. Combining these data points, Element451 calculates applicants' probability of enrolling, successfully graduating, and becoming a loyal alumna and the likely sum of financial aid they might need and request. Another such software, Kira Talent, is a Canadian-developed system that scores applicants on a five-point Likert scale on agreeableness, motivation, neuroticism, and openness, based on a video that the applicant has submitted. Artificial intelligence thus helps university admissions to understand what applicant profiles are most likely to succeed in the admissions process and who are most likely to accept an offer from a university, are most likely to complete their studies, and most importantly, have a prosperous professional career after graduating. This facilitates the evaluation and adjusting of admission tests and procedures in place, as well as serving as decision help for human recruiters making the final decision on whether to admit an applicant (Kadiu 2021; Newton 2021).

Now supposing the admissions office's AI was mistaken when predicting an applicant's success at the institution. In that case, AI can serve as an early warning system and detect applicants who are likely to run into difficulties at university. Identifying struggling students as early as possible can be highly valuable to providing them with the necessary support and consequently increase student retention. For example, Staffordshire University supports students with Beacon, an AI-powered teaching assistant, which recommends readings and further learning resources and connects students with (human) tutors (Larsson 2019). Moreover, AI can significantly improve learning and teaching by applying learning analytics, which are output from students' data evaluation, allowing for pedagogical approaches such as adaptive learning (Carbonell 1970), with the degree of difficulty and pace adapted to each learner consistent with their previous knowledge, personal learning capacities, and so forth.

Covid-19 especially led to an acceleration and a stepping-up of higher education's digital transformation. In many cases, it was not until the outbreak of the pandemic that universities and the higher education sector began to be familiarized with learning analytics and how to apply them. For educators, learning analytics enable supervising a learner's progress, giving an overview of what pedagogical material is used and by whom, and finally, improving and adjusting course content and teaching approach. For students, learning analytics enables them to track their learning progress and their potential improvement in a specific subject and to compare themselves to fellow students. Adaptive learning uses such learning analytics and applies AI systems to customize the student's profile. Adaptive learning thus supports student-centricity, significantly improving the learning experience. Moreover, personalized teaching significantly reduces dropout rates (Kaplan 2021b; Kaplan and Pucciarelli 2016; Pucciarelli and Kaplan 2016, 2017).

If a student's course corrections have led to the desired learning outcome, it is usually reflected in final exams, where here too artificial intelligence can be instrumental (Labayen 2021). Pennsylvania State University, for example, uses AI-driven Examity to prevent exam cheating in an online environment, that is, when students cannot be monitored in a physical setting, but surveillance needs to take place remotely. Examity applies predictive analytics, biometric keystroke identification, and video supervision to confirm a learner's identity. Even grading can be done with the help of AI. At Southern New Hampshire University, AI helps to grade vast numbers of exams in a reasonable turnaround time. During Covid-19, universities worldwide were compelled to operate entirely online, examinations included, which led to significant problems of not ensuring that testing is secure. However, this is primordial to certify a student's quality and readiness for the job market. AI might be just the answer in the university of the 21st century (Kaplan 2021b).

The use of such surveillance techniques and the analysis of a multitude of students' data naturally raises concerns about data protection and privacy (Roberts et al. 2020). A look at the Chinese higher education landscape hints at necessary limits and considerations (Chan 2018). Several of China's universities and schools are equipped with security cameras in classrooms and auditoriums to detect students' emotions during class, differentiating among options such as anger, disgruntlement, pleasure, sadness, fear, surprise, or neutral. Facial expressions reveal whether students are engaged, understand the lecture, or are bored, in the latter case with the professor immediately being prompted to take measures to make the class more engaging. Moreover, cameras automatically note a student's attendance and detect what students are doing at any given time, that is, listening, reading, talking, or writing. Facial recognition is also applied in the cafeterias and libraries, eliminating the need for meal plan and library cards. Some universities and schools also fit their students' uniforms with RFID tags to constantly surveil where they are and what they are doing (Caiyu 2018). China pursues such a monitoring and control system not only in the academic sector, but more broadly in society at large, as we will discuss in Chapter 5.

Presently, AI is mainly used to improve teaching quality, simplify educators' lives, and free up faculty from paperwork and repeatedly responding to students' queries, enabling them to engage in higher-value activities such as coaching, mentoring, and research. Even in the latter, AI can be of use: The British RELX Group, Elsevier's mother company, uses artificial intelligence to automate the writing of scientific literature reviews, the assessment of potential data forgery and plagiarism, and much more. While human educators and researchers are still needed, in light of the aforementioned evolutions and developments, we can legitimately ask when AI will replace humans as pedagogues. Think how this generation of humanized AI applications (cf. Chapter 2) could transform the higher education sector: Essentially, they could become the instructors. High salaries for human faculty might render AI systems appealing in higher education, which increasingly finds itself under financial pressure.

Of course, we also have to ask whether students would agree to be taught by machines, and if such an impersonal approach could succeed. Regardless, higher education will certainly need to reflect upon these questions and take measures to be ready for such changes across the sector. Meanwhile, there is no doubt that teachers should take an interest in adapting to the digital environment, applying learning analytics, making use of adaptive learning, and generally changing their way of doing things (Zawacki-Richter et al. 2019). Whatever Artificial Intelligence's effect on Higher Education, it certainly is both Absolutely Intriguing and Hugely Exciting.

b. Both blessing and curse? AI in the workplace

Even if currently "not yet ready for prime time," self-driving cars are invariably cited as a prime example of AI applications with many, if not all, of the major automobile manufactures working on their development in one way or another (The Economist 2020). Looking at Tesla's autopilot function or Google's self-driving car endeavor, we see that it is likely only a matter of time until the roads are full of these intelligent vehicles. The Covid-19 pandemic forced the workforce into home offices, prompting us to rethink both the workplace and commuting. Self-driving vehicles could push this concept even further, providing employees the possibility of being conducted to work, during which they could already begin their workday on the road. Alongside smart cars, AI also leads to smart (home) offices that learn employees' behavior and work routines, using this information to help employers save energy, water, and of course money. Employees' workplace experience in general will change with AI systems and AI-driven robots becoming co-workers in offices, warehouses, and manufacturing plants worldwide (Wilson and Daugherty 2018). These are just some of many examples of how AI might change the workplace.

Looking at more direct business applications of AI, we can cite KLM Royal Dutch Airlines as an illustration (Kaplan 2020c). With over 130,000 weekly mentions on the broad range of its social media accounts and more than 30,000 actual customer queries, KLM decided to apply AI to automate responding, at least to passengers' common questions. This freed up valuable time for the (human) employees to invest their working hours on more challenging and complex demands. Approximately half of KLM's customer inquiries are now processed and finalized by artificial intelligence. For the remaining half, the system provides possible answers to its human counterparts, again facilitating their task. Learning from the human employees' answers and reactions, the system steadily improves over time, capable of replacing more and more of the human workforce or increasingly able to help them, depending upon which semantic we apply.

The KLM case is just one small example of automation and artificial intelligence drastically transforming the workplace, work tasks, and future job opportunities. PricewaterhouseCoopers (PwC; Rao and Verweij 2017), for example, conducted a study of 200,000 companies showing that by the early 2020s, approximately 3% of employment is at risk of automation. This number rises to 20% by 2031. By the mid-2030s, it could reach 30%. For lower-skilled employment, it might increase to nearly half of current jobs.

Such automation and replacement will necessarily lead to mass unemployment in various sectors, with commensurate social tensions. The same study (Rao and Verweij 2017) cites a possible $15 trillion increase in the world's gross domestic product by the year 2030 due to AI and society's digitalization. It is yet to be seen whether job creations will offset AI-induced unemployment. What is certain is that massive shifts in job markets will take place (Kaplan and Haenlein 2020), consistent with what John Keynes predicted almost a century ago: "We are being afflicted with a new disease of which some readers may not have heard the name, but of which they will hear a great deal in the years to come—namely, technological unemployment" (Keynes 1930, p. 37).

Alongside these job markets shifts—simultaneously representing a blessing and curse depending on the eye of the beholder—when considering AI in the workplace, we furthermore need to look at technological, legal, and ethical concerns. Regarding technical considerations, Raji and Buolamwini's (2019) work shows that Amazon's facial recognition software exhibited significant gender and racial discrimination: Darker-complected females were wrongly classified as males in more than 30% of cases, while the same AI system erred thusly in fewer than 10% of cases concerning lighter-complected females. Men, on the other hand, were correctly categorized in all cases. Of course, Amazon did not consciously plan for this; its AI system simply learned to recognize light-complected men, leading to the described bias and incorrect classifications. Microsoft's Twitter chatbot, named Tay, serves as a further example (Hunt 2016): Tay followed Twitter discussions to learn from them and consequently participate in them. Manipulated by online trolls feeding Tay their conversations and data, Tay rapidly turned into a bigoted, misogynous, strongly offensive chatbot. Example Tay tweets were: "We're going to build a wall, and Mexico's going to pay for it" or "I . . . hate feminists, and they should all die and burn in hell."

Such technical concerns quickly transform into legal ones, questioning transparency, liability, or predictability. Continuing with Amazon for illustration purposes, suppose a child orders an upscale dollhouse via the brand's virtual assistant, Alexa. This actually happened: As her parents couldn't afford the item, a local TV channel thought the story interesting enough to report it. The news anchor, at some point, enthusiastically reported the child saying, "Alexa ordered me a dollhouse" (Earl 2017). This phrase was subsequently heard by Alexas in multiple kitchens and living rooms, which tried to buy these $170 dollhouses. Although no such orders were approved, this anecdote well illustrates the potential legal nightmares untangling who is liable in such situations. To decide such questions would demand algorithmic transparency, that is, know exactly how Amazon's shopping algorithm works. However, for at least two reasons, algorithmic transparency might be challenging to attain: On the one hand, the algorithm doubtlessly has the highest value of all components of an AI system, so that companies are naturally reluctant to share their details thereon. On the other hand, the company might not even know itself how the algorithm works, as by definition AI develops and learns independently, leading to a black box situation. To potentially be unable to disclose a system's algorithm will doubtlessly give plenty of headaches (and money) to attorneys, judges, and other personnel (Kaplan and Haenlein 2020).

Finally, the workplace will also have to tackle several ethical dilemmas and concerns. Just think of the marketing domain, for example, and the vast amount of personal data available to marketers, enabling them to forecast customers' purchasing behavior, desires, and addictions. Should one sell high-calorie food to obese people, any kind of drugs to an expectant mother, or luxury products to those in debt? AI systems can pinpoint such consumer characteristics to nearly 100% accuracy by analyzing past behavior and data. Does an enterprise have the ethical obligation to take such information into account? Does it have the right? This is just one more example of why artificial intelligence might simultaneously represent a blessing and a curse in the workplace and the economy (Kaplan 2020b).

c. Might AI become a threat to democracy . . . or is it already?

About ten years ago, social media applications were proclaimed as giving back influence to citizens (Kaplan and Haenlein 2010, Kaplan 2012), empowering them, and constituting a booster for democracy. Just look at the Arab Spring protests and uprisings spread across much of the Arab world in the early 2010s, many said. Citizens destabilized a number of undemocratic regimes by disseminating their opposition on social media, organizing demonstrations, and even starting entire revolutions resulting in bringing down their governments. Yet, in the last decade, social media, upgraded by artificial intelligence, went from being a booster to a severe threat to democracy (Kaplan 2020a). Social media are increasingly applied to disseminate misinformation, or fake news, to manipulate entire citizenries. Moreover, deepfakes, which are authentic-looking videos where the subject appears to say things they actually have not said and most likely would never say in reality, are disseminated for the same purpose. Russian manipulation efforts via fake news against Hillary Clinton in the 2016 US electoral race, resulting in Donald Trump winning the election, were widely reported. Also, in several other elections, such as those of Austria, France, Germany, and Italy, evidence arose of Russia interfering with voter outcomes via targeted misinformation disseminated on social media (Kamarck

2018). Just imagine if Russia could produce legitimate-looking audio and video content in addition to text-based communication to enhance their misinformation campaign. In fact, not much imagination is necessary, as it is already feasible.

At least three domains wherein AI can be a threat to democracy exist. Besides the aforementioned possibility of manipulation, AI can also be used for citizen surveillance, and finally, AI-generated frustration could keep potential voters from voting (Kaplan 2020a). Concerning manipulation, AI-boosted social media can easily be used to influence citizens' voting behavior. Generally speaking, social media use algorithms that provide content adapted to users consistent with their online behavior and preferences. If, for example, you're a cat fancier, you probably "like" many cat images. The algorithm will learn this and show you more cats on your social media feed. Ultimately, you might see nearly exclusively . . . cute cats. This example is true not only of pets or hobbies, but also (political) ideas and views. Being exposed to the same opinions repeatedly, citizens eventually get the impression that everybody shares the same line of thinking, as they no longer see any opposing views. As people increasingly use social media as their sole information channel, without drawing news from news outlets, ultimately the only thing a citizen knows is what s/he sees on social media.

While this manipulation is a mere effect of the functioning of social media and its algorithms, conscious and targeted manipulation exists, either by stretching the truth to the maximum or by blatantly lying. In the first case, hyper-targeting is applied to customize information to specific citizen groups. Essentially, various voter segments are provided with communications that the algorithms deduce that they would enjoy receiving. As such, everybody gets what they want to read, hear, or watch. Going even a step further leads to the aforementioned fake news or deepfakes: False and incorrect information is disseminated about a political candidate, cause, or product on social media. Such methods' effectiveness can be measured by looking at the pre-election period of the 2016 US election: During the final three months of the campaign, the top 20 fake news items on Facebook garnered more likes, shares, and comments than did the 20 most-read items from 19 leading news outlets combined (such as the *New York Times* and the Huffington Post). Moreover, approximately 75% of those who consumed such fake news believed it to be authentic (Silverman 2016).

Concerning surveillance, a look at the US police shows the power of artificial intelligence in such an endeavor and its endangering potential for democracies. Applying AI, the US police can predict when and where potential crime might occur, accordingly sending a patrol to these areas at the respective times. Even names of likely victims or perpetrators are provided and identified by the AI system's algorithm. Police can take actions accordingly, such as informing potential victims of danger and potential perpetrators that they are identified as such and under more scrutiny. However, we need to be careful with such measures. As with Amazon's racially biased face detection algorithm, unfortunately such bias is possible not only in the consumer domain; the US police algorithm, trained in prior cases, identified African-Americans as far more prone to engage in illegal behavior than those of other ethnicities (Portilho 2019). This example indicates the possibility of artificial intelligence constituting a threat to freedom in any democracy, not to mention non-democratic regimes (cf. Chapter 5c: "China: the ultimate AI trAIning ground").

Finally, alongside manipulation and supervision, AI-induced citizen behavior represents a further threat to democracy: Not knowing what is genuine and fake, citizens might be tempted to abandon participation in political life; voters become non-voters. The more difficult the verification of content becomes and the more deceptive behavior occurs, the more likely it is that citizens' trust in their political institutions will diminish. As analyzed by several studies, Donald Trump became president not as a result of a higher voter turnout of non-college-educated Caucasians than in previous elections (the explanation that the Trump team claimed to be the reason for his election win), but due to a sharp decrease in African-American voter turnout (Kamarck 2018). According to the Robert Mueller report, "The Russians allegedly masqueraded as African-American and Muslim activists to urge minority voters to abstain from voting in the 2016 election or to vote for a third-party candidate" (Mosk, Turner, and Faulders 2018). Fake social media accounts pretending to be African-Americans convinced actual African-Americans to "Choose peace and vote for Jill Stein" or boycott the election altogether, that is, "We'd surely be better off not voting AT ALL" (Mosk, Turner, and Faulders 2018). This explains some (if not all) of the reasons for fewer African-Americans voting than in earlier elections.

In the next chapter, we will see what we can do to overcome AI's threat to democracy. Ultimately, artificial intelligence constitutes both a danger and a boon to democracy, depending on how it is applied, and obviously by whom. We even can go a step further, putting our fate entirely in the hand of machines and abandoning human political representation altogether. An AI-powered system could continually collect data on a society's current opinions and preferences. Policy would reflect in-the-moment public interests, potentially drawing a more precise picture than that in which politicians and parties are in office for several years, possibly shifting further away from current opinions with time. It might not even be necessary to poll the citizenry on the relevant topics. Youyou, Kosinski, and Stillwell (2015), for example, found that machine-driven judgments of an individual's personality are more accurate than are assessments made by humans. Ten likes of an individual and the prediction of her preferences as calculated by Facebook's algorithm will largely outperform predictions by that individual's coworker. Only 150 likes, and AI outperforms family members. Three hundred likes, and the algorithm will likely outperform the individual's spouse. But would we trust such a machine-based decision process? People already trust algorithms when considering apps telling them which political candidate or party is closest to their preferences. Compared to human politicians, one could argue that machines, which are unbiased by personal interests, narcissism, or ideological beliefs, are more rational and evidence-based. At least this appears to be the impression of a non-negligible group of people based on a study by the Center for the Governance of Change at Spain's IE University (Jonsson and de Tena 2019). Approximately one quarter of 2,500 respondents from across Europe preferred decision-making by AI over human politicians, certainly giving us food for thought (Kaplan 2020a, 2020c).

References

Caiyu, Liu (2018) Chinese Schools Monitor Students Activities, Targeting Truancy with 'Intelligent Uniforms', *Global Times*, December 20.

Carbonell, Jaime R. (1970) AI in CAI: An Artificial Intelligence Approach to Computer Aided Instruction, *IEEE Transactions on Man-Machine Systems*, 11(4), 190–202.

Chan, Francis Tara (2018) A School in China Is Monitoring Students with Facial-Recognition Technology That Scans the Classroom Every 30 Seconds, *Insider*, May 21.

Earl, Jennifer (2017) TV News Anchor's Report Accidentally Sets Off Viewers' Amazon Echo Dots, *CBS News*, January 10.

The Economist (2020) Driverless Cars Show the Limits of Today's AI: They, and Many Other Such Systems, Still Struggle to Handle the Unexpected, *The Economist*, June 13.

Haenlein, Michael, Kaplan Andreas (2019) A Brief History of AI: On the Past, Present, and Future of Artificial Intelligence, *California Management Review*, 61(4), 5–14.

Hunt, Elle (2016) Tay, Microsoft's AI Chatbot, Gets a Crash Course in Racism from Twitter: Attempt to Engage Millennials with Artificial Intelligence Backfires Hours after Launch, with TayTweets Account Citing Hitler and Supporting Donald Trump, *The Guardian*, March 24.

Jonsson, Oscar, de Tena Carlos Luca (2019) European Tech Insights Mapping European Attitudes towards Technological Change and Its Governance, Center for the Governance of Change, IE.

Kadiu, Ardis (2021) Pre- and Post-COVID, Technology Is Reshaping Admissions Forever, *Inside HigherEd*, April 15.

Kamarck, Elaine (2018) Malevolent Soft Power, AI, and the Threat to Democracy, in *A Blueprint for the Future of AI*. Washington, DC: The Brookings Institution.

Kaplan, Andreas (2012) If You Love Something, Let It Go Mobile: Mobile Marketing and Mobile Social Media 4×4, *Business Horizons*, 55(2), 129–139.

Kaplan, Andreas (2020a) Artificial Intelligence, Social Media, and Fake News: Is This the End of Democracy?, in Gül, A. A., Ertürk, Y. D. and Elmer, P. (eds.), *Digital Transformation in Media and Society*. Istanbul, Turkey: Istanbul University Press Books, 149–161.

Kaplan, Andreas (2020b) Artificial Intelligence, Marketing, and the Fourth Industrial Revolution: Clarifications, Challenges, Concerns, in Christiansen, B. and Škrinjarić, T. (eds.), *Handbook of Research on Applied AI for International Business and Marketing Applications*. Hershey, Pennsylvania: IGI, 1–13.

Kaplan, Andreas (2020c) Social Media Powered by Artificial Intelligence, Violence and Nonviolence, in Kurtz, L. (ed.), *Encyclopedia of Violence, Peace & Conflict* (3rd ed.). Cambridge, MA: Elsevier.

Kaplan, Andreas (2021a) Artificial Intelligence (AI): When Humans and Machines Might Have to Coexist, in Verdegem, P. (ed.), *AI for Everyone? Critical Perspectives*. London: University of Westminster Press, 21–32.

Kaplan, Andreas (2021b) *Higher Education at the Crossroads of Disruption: The University of the 21st Century, Great Debates in Higher Education*. Bingley, UK: Emerald Publishing.

Kaplan, Andreas (2021c) Your Attention, Please: You've Got 15 Seconds! TikTok and How Organizations Can Make Use of It, in Kolukirik, S. (ed.), *Digitalization and Future of Digital Society*. Berlin, Germany: Peter Lang Publishing House, 367–378.

Kaplan, Andreas (2022) *Digital Transformation and Disruption of Higher Education*. Cambridge: Cambridge University Press.

Kaplan, Andreas, Haenlein Michael (2010) Users of the World, Unite! The Challenges and Opportunities of Social Media, *Business Horizons*, 53(1), 59–68.

Kaplan, Andreas, Haenlein Michael (2011) The Early Bird Catches the News: Nine Things You Should Know about Micro-Blogging, *Business Horizons*, 54(2), 105–113.

Kaplan, Andreas, Haenlein Michael (2019) Siri, Siri in My Hand, Who Is the Fairest in the Land? On the Interpretations, Illustrations and Implications of Artificial Intelligence, *Business Horizons*, 62(1), 15–25.

Kaplan, Andreas, Haenlein Michael (2020) Rulers of the World, Unite! The Challenges and Opportunities of Artificial Intelligence, *Business Horizons*, 63(1), 37–50.

Kaplan, Andreas, Pucciarelli Francesca (2016) Contemporary Challenges in Higher Education: Three E's for Education: Enhance, Embrace, Expand, IAU HORIZONS, *International Universities Bureau of the United Nations*, 21(4), 25–26.

Keynes, John M. (1930) Economic Possibilities for Our Grandchildren, in Keynes, J. M. (ed.), *Essays in Persuasion*. London, UK: Macmillan.

Labayen, Mikel, Vea Ricardo, Florez Julian, Aginako Naiara, Sierra Basilio (2021) Online Student Authentication and Proctoring System Based on Multimodal Biometrics Technology, *IEEE Access*, 9, 72398–72411.

Larsson, Naomi (2019) 'It's an Educational Revolution': How AI Is Transforming University Life: AI Chatbots Have Arrived on UK University Campuses: But Is the Hype Justified?, *The Guardian*, April 17.

Leopold, Todd (2017) A Professor Built an AI Teaching Assistant for His Courses: And It Could Shape the Future of Education, *Business Insider*, March 22.

McFarland, Matt (2016) What Happened When a Professor Built a Chatbot to Be His Teaching Assistant, *The Washington Post*, May 11.

Mosk, Matthew, Turner Trish, Faulders Katherine (2018) Russian Influence Operation Attempted to Suppress Black Vote: Indictment, *ABC News*, February 18.

Newton, Derek (2021) From Admissions to Teaching to Grading, AI Is Infiltrating Higher Education: As Colleges' Use of the Technology Grows, So Do Questions about Bias and Accuracy, *The Hechinger Report*, April 26.

Portilho, Thais (2019) The Consequences of Our Blind Faith in Artificial Intelligence Are Catching Up to Us, *The Independent*, March 24.

Pucciarelli, Francesca, Kaplan Andreas (2016) Competition and Strategy in Higher Education: Managing Complexity and Uncertainty, *Business Horizons*, 59(3), 311–320.

Pucciarelli, Francesca, Kaplan Andreas (2017) Le Università Europee oggi: sfide e nuove strategie, *Economia & Management*, gennaio/febbraio, (1), 85–95.

Raji, Inioluwa D., Buolamwini Joy (2019) Actionable Auditing: Investigating the Impact of Publicly Naming Biased Performance Results of Commercial AI Products, Conference on Artificial Intelligence, Ethics, and Society, Honolulu, January 27–28.

Rao, Anand S., Verweij Gerard (2017) Sizing the Prize-What's the Real Value of AI for Your Business and How Can You Capitalise?, PricewaterhouseCoopers.

Roberts, Huw, Cowls Josh, Morley Jessica, Taddeo Mariarosaria, Wang Vincent, Floridi Luciano (2020) The Chinese Approach to Artificial Intelligence: An Analysis of Policy, Ethics, and Regulation, AI & Society.

Silverman, Craig (2016) This Analysis Shows How Viral Fake Election News Stories Outperformed Real News on Facebook, *Buzzfeed*, November 16.

Wilson, James H., Daugherty Paul R. (2018) Collaborative Intelligence: Humans and AI Are Joining Forces, Humans and Machines Can Enhance Each Other's Strengths, *Harvard Business Review*, July/August, 114–123.

Youyou, Wu, Kosinski Michal, Stillwell David (2015) Computer-Based Personality Judgments Are More Accurate Than Those Made by Humans, *Proceedings of the National Academy of Sciences*, 112(4), 1036–1040.

Zawacki-Richter, Olaf, Marín Victoria I., Bond Melissa, Gouverneur Franziska (2019) Systematic Review of Research on Artificial Intelligence Applications in Higher Education: Where Are the Educators?, *International Journal of Educational Technology in Higher Education*, 16, 39.

4 Constructions

Preparing for the AI Revolution

AI progress is rapid, its influence across society is increasingly apparent, and we need to prepare for the AI Revolution. Three possible ways of constructing a future in a world characterized by AI progress are presented and analyzed. First, light will be shed on the state's role in designing regulation that prevents AI from endangering human rights, erects barriers to AI-induced wrongdoing while simultaneously fostering innovation and investments, and creates and protects the labor market. Another way to prepare society to better deal with artificial intelligence lies in education leading to AI literacy, and strengthening ethical conduct within the nation's leadership and elite. This chapter thus explains how education and ethics are an absolute imperative in this new era, to establish the proper approach and attitude regarding artificial intelligence, its opportunities and threats. Moreover, regional and cultural differences regarding AI will be presented, underscoring the necessity for international collaboration and cooperation. In particular, we will look at the world's artificial intelligence superpowers— the US and China—as well as the European Union, which is considered as significantly lagging behind them in AI research and development (Kaplan and Haenlein 2020).

a. Regulation and the role of the state

When thinking of how society can prepare for the AI Revolution, the state comes to mind first. While regulation is undoubtedly necessary, regulating AI is not a simple endeavor. In many cases, regulating a market constitutes a barrier to invention and creativity. With AI likely forging the future employment market, any given country will have a strong interest in AI innovation and development occurring on its soil, pointing to a relatively liberal approach to artificial intelligence. Currently, GAFAM (i.e., Google, Amazon, Facebook, Apple, and Microsoft) in the US and BAT (i.e., Baidu, Alibaba, and Tencent) in China, together with the Chinese government,

DOI: 10.4324/9781003244554-4

dominate AI's evolutionary progress. As aforementioned, AI demands a large quantity of data from which algorithms can learn and thereby improve their performance and accuracy. Data protection and privacy concerns are (so far) of less concern in the US than in other countries and minimal in China, which explains these two countries' AI predominance (Kaplan and Haenlein 2020).

This tradeoff between regulation and innovation is also the concern of the European Union, which aims for a humane approach to artificial intelligence when establishing a legal framework for AI, which is one of many attempts worldwide to organize and control AI's evolution. When the European Commission (2021) published its Regulation on Artificial Intelligence in April 2021, the objective was to provide a basis for a legal (and ethical) framework that protects citizens' rights while at the same time fostering innovation as well as investment in AI on EU territory. Often considered the new General Data Protection Regulation (GDPR) for AI, it would apply to the European Union and countries external to EU borders if the respective AI system is put on Europe's market or affects those residing in the EU. The regulatory framework applies to actors regardless of where they are located, and therefore might influence AI regulation worldwide, as is the case with GDPR.

The logic behind the EU regulation is based on the degree of risk that a given AI system potentially represents. Various measures and requirements apply depending on the categories—"unacceptable risk," "high risk," "limited risk," or "minimal risk"—into which a given system falls. In the case of AI systems presenting unacceptable risk, defined as AI contravening EU values and violating fundamental rights, are simply not allowed. More precisely, the regulation states that unacceptable risk AI are those

> that have a significant potential to manipulate persons through subliminal techniques beyond their consciousness or exploit vulnerabilities of specific vulnerable groups such as children or persons with disabilities to materially distort their behaviour in a manner that is likely to cause them or another person psychological or physical harm.

Moreover, the regulation explicitly bans "AI-based social scoring for general purposes done by public authorities" as well as the "use of real-time remote biometric identification systems in publicly accessible spaces for law enforcement [purposes]" (European Commission 2021). The prohibition on social scoring can certainly be interpreted as a direct attack against China's scoring system (see Chapter 5c). The interdiction of biometric identification possibly responds to concerns about facial recognition systems allowing authorities to match images of unknown persons to pictures of them found online. This procedure exists in the United States and has already elicited strong critique from the European Union. Noncompliance fines can reach €30 million or 6% of yearly turnover, whichever is the more significant amount to the perpetrator. Compare this to the maximum 4% of annual turnover in the case of GDPR noncompliance, and you can understand the seriousness and importance the EU places on regulating artificial intelligence.

Alongside the EU, several other regions in the world have begun regulating AI. The US Federal Trade Commission (FTC) based its guidelines on "truth, fairness, and equity," applying the rule of thumb that any AI that "causes more harm than good" should be prohibited. Obviously, this leaves much room for interpretation. Although the various regulations differ in their nuances because regulators disagree on what exactly AI is (see Chapter 2 on the importance of clearly defining AI), three broad commonalities can be identified (Burt 2021): The first, applied to the EU's regulation, is the requirement to assess the risk involved in a given AI system, referred to as "algorithmic impact assessment," or "IA for AI." The second commonality is accountability and independence, which requires that an AI system and its potential danger be evaluated by third-party, independent data scientists, lawyers, and others who do not have any vested interest in the system being assessed. The third commonality requires ongoing assessment, that is, regular testing of AI systems that might have changed and evolved by themselves over time, as per the definition of AI. The latter implicitly means that we never can be certain of the exact risk posed by a given AI system other than at the precise moment of risk evaluation.

Alongside regulating AI systems directly, governments are increasingly taking measures concerning the job markets that are or will be affected by automation and AI. Massive unemployment, at least for certain (lower qualification) professions, is likely. Call centers, for example, will almost certainly be staffed with AI-driven chatbots. But AI will also profoundly influence high-qualification jobs. Studies show that engineers', attorneys', and radiologists' jobs may be susceptible to advances in AI and might well be replaced by machines (Huang and Rust 2018). An initial solution might be for governments to compel organizations to limit automation to retain jobs. France, for example, enacted laws requiring electronic platforms in the civil service to run only during regular office hours, that is, to be shut down outside of these hours. A longer-term approach would of course be to train, re-skill, and up-skill the workforce to enable its members to move into jobs less vulnerable to AI's effect (Kaplan and Haenlein 2020; cf. Section 4b on Education).

While continuing education and lifelong learning are the way to go, not everyone is either willing or able to engage therein, and unemployment will hit many sectors regardless. One way to allow workers to remain at least partly employed might be to redistribute the total amount of working hours, for example a four-day workweek, or limit weekly working hours to 30. At some point, governments will have to confront the concept of guaranteed income, which is already a hot topic in some countries. For example, in Finland's case, guaranteed income has been shown to be less efficient than predicted, at least as was designed by the Finnish government (Kaplan and Haenlein 2020).

Regulators and legislators worldwide will need to look into many different areas, with progress in automation, digitalization, and artificial intelligence often taking place faster than policy is crafted, enacted, and implemented. Regarding the previous chapter's discussion of AI representing a possible danger to democracy, several directions have already been taken: The Anti-Information Manipulation Act, enacted by France in 2018, requires social media platforms to explicitly flag content where sponsorship exceeds €100 and indicate the sponsor's identity. The same law enables expedited judicial decisions in case of manipulative content or fake news intended to influence an election outcome. However, most countries still count on self-regulation by social media, which have taken steps to identify and remove fake news and deepfakes. Some methods entail the implementation of human or non-human fact checkers, flagging false or misleading information, providing (truthful) counter-information, or shutting down fake or bot-run accounts. Facebook's attempts to do so, for example, show that such measures are more complicated than we thought. After having begun flagging potentially fake news, Facebook rapidly switched to demoting, that is, not giving prominence to potentially false information on users' feeds, labeling potential fake news and deepfakes with red flags. Yet even if confirmed, eradicating misinformation was not an option for Facebook, as it could be considered an attack on free speech (Kaplan 2020).

b. AI literacy and ethical conduct

To co-exist with machines, human beings must acquire AI literacy, that is, master a series of competencies and skills enabling us to understand and assess AI systems critically. People must also engage and collaborate with artificially intelligent machines and robots effectively, that is, develop a comprehension throughout the population of how AI works and functions. Just as it is helpful to know some Italian phrases and a bit of Italian culture if you want to do business in Italy, it is equally beneficial—even imperative— to know the basics of programming as well as algorithmics when regularly interacting with digital entities, which today means nearly everywhere we turn: the ATM, the supermarket, the customer call center.

Moreover, technical competencies must be accompanied by soft skill mastery. According to the World Economic Forum (2016), nine out of ten skills required in the future will be nontechnical in nature: creativity, critical thinking, emotional intelligence, and personnel management specifically. The same line of thinking is found in "Lead the Leap," the UNESCO (2019) report on AI, which states that the educational sector should focus not only on technological competencies, but also on human-centric skills. Moreover, flexibility, adaptability, and certainly also entrepreneurship will be useful in the era of artificial intelligence (Kaplan 2021b). Openness to lifelong learning is, without a doubt, an imperative. Only by continuously up- and re-skilling will we be able to adapt to new contexts and working realities, to cope with and adjust to the constantly changing world affected by advances in AI. Education today must be designed with ever-increasing human / machine interplay in mind (Kaplan 2021a, 2022).

Regarding fake news and deepfakes disseminated on social media, education inarguably has an essential role. This is illustrated by a study conducted by the Max Planck Institute for Informatics wherein real videos and deepfakes of Theresa May, Barack Obama, and Vladimir Putin were shown to participants (Kim et al. 2018), over half of whom believed the fake videos to be real. Moreover, only 80% believed the real videos to be authentic. It is incumbent on all of us to be aware of how social media can be misused for manipulation and to be keenly conscious of data security, privacy concerns, and challenges induced by big data and its use. Aside from regulations or technological ways of identifying fake news, ultimately it is we who decide what to believe or reject. To that end, Stony Brook University School of Journalism has developed a news literacy program wherein students learn to differentiate between fact and fake and between information, promotion, and entertainment. Also, ESCP Business School (European School of Commerce in Paris), has introduced dedicated courses on AI and its likely effect on society into several of its study programs. Search engine giant Google likewise launched an initiative to enhance and teach digital literacy (Schindler 2018).

In this regard, we cannot forget those who are past the age of attending school or university: They need to hit the books again (or rather enroll in massive open online courses (MOOCs) and small private online course (SPOC); Kaplan and Haenlein 2016) and become AI ready, especially regarding elections. An excellent example of what such training and education looks like is to be found in the Netherlands. Shortly before the 2019 elections for European Parliament, the Netherlands launched an online campaign educating Dutch citizens about fake news and the possibility of it being used to try to affect the electoral outcome. The campaign's website, for example, explained:

Disinformation and fake news are a big problem in other countries. There are many different media in the Netherlands, showing various angles of the news. Therefore, fake news and disinformation in the Netherlands do not yet have much influence. But the government wants to prevent their occurring. Everyone in the Netherlands must remain critical and curious about where their news comes from. Read these tips for recognizing the difference between fake and real news.

(Dutch Government 2018)

While education is necessary for civilization to be AI ready, it is not sufficient. AI does whatever it has been programmed to do. The danger begins when unethical individuals issue the orders and explicitly aim at illegal, harmful, or otherwise nefarious objectives. Ethical leadership thus becomes more imperative than ever, as the stakes are now higher. Accordingly, teaching ethical decision-making is critical to any society's future. Such ethics classes must be in every curriculum, whatever the discipline (Kaplan 2021b). While regulation and policies can certainly work to enforce and supervise ethical behavior, we also need to think about the legislator's ethical conduct. What happens when the regulators themselves apply artificial intelligence in ways that are questionable from a moral point of view? China and its application of artificial intelligence can serve as an example thereof and will be analyzed in detail in Chapter 5.

To cover all of our bases, another issue regarding AI and ethics needs mention. Assigning a task to an AI system clearly and precisely, so as not to lead to any mishaps, is not as easy as it sounds. In fact, we humans are imprecise creatures, counting on our fellow humans to correctly interpret our statements and share our value system and ethical framework. AI, however, does not (yet) possess such interpretation skills. For example, imagine an AI system asked to take over the protection and security of French president Emmanuel Macron. What is more secure than just putting him into the Élysée Palace and not letting him step outside? Although this most likely was not the AI system commander's intention, incarcerating an individual without cause being highly unethical, this is possibly the most rational way of obeying such an order. To correctly interpret human beings' orders and commands, AI needs to develop a comprehension of ethics and norms, such as the general principle of proportionality. However, to do so might not be an easy endeavor and is all the more complicated as values, norms, and ethics are culturally forged and differ across societies (as will be discussed in this chapter's final section).

To see an example of what such guidelines might look like, let's turn to the European Union. The EU Commission's High-Level Expert Group on

Artificial Intelligence suggests in their Ethics Guidelines for Trustworthy AI (2019) that AI systems must be lawful (compliant with current regulations and laws), ethical (respect human values and principles), and robust (technically sound, taking into account their social context). More precisely, seven requirements were set forth:

1   Human agency and oversight: AI systems should empower human beings, allowing them to make informed decisions, and foster their fundamental rights. At the same time, proper oversight mechanisms need to be ensured, which can be achieved through human-in-the-loop, human-on-the-loop, and human-in-command approaches.

2   Technical robustness and safety: AI systems need to be resilient and secure. They need to be safe, ensuring a fallback plan in case something goes wrong, as well as being accurate, reliable, and reproducible. This is the only way to ensure that unintentional harm can be minimized and prevented.

3   Privacy and data governance: Besides ensuring full respect for privacy and data protection, adequate data governance mechanisms must also be secure, taking into account the quality and integrity of the data, and ensuring legitimised access to data.

4   Transparency: The data, system, and AI business models should be transparent, which traceability mechanisms can help achieve. Moreover, AI systems and their decisions should be explained in a manner comprehensible to the stakeholder concerned. Humans need to be aware that they are interacting with an AI system, and must be informed of the system's capabilities and limitations.

5   Diversity, non-discrimination, and fairness: Unfair bias must be avoided, as it could have multiple negative implications, from the marginalization of vulnerable groups, to the exacerbation of prejudice and discrimination. Fostering diversity, AI systems should be accessible to all, regardless of any disability, and involve relevant stakeholders throughout their entire life circle.

6   Societal and environmental well-being: AI systems should benefit all human beings, including future generations. It must hence be ensured that they are sustainable and environmentally friendly. Moreover, they should take into account the environment, including other living creatures, and their social and societal impact should be carefully considered.

7   Accountability: Mechanisms should be in place to ensure responsibility and accountability for AI systems and their outcomes. Auditability, which enables the assessment of algorithms, data, and design processes,

plays a key role therein, especially in critical applications. Moreover, adequate and accessible redress should be ensured.

(European Commission 2019)

c. International relations and cross-cultural cooperation

As aforementioned, AI development and progress are currently occurring mainly in China and the US, both of whom have begun engaging in a cold tech war with each other. For the moment, it is unclear who will come out as the winner. In China, AI is primarily controlled and supervised by the state, which aims, inter alia, to boost the Chinese economy; while in the US, AI is advanced mainly by private companies pursuing corporate prosperity. In particular, the Chinese government's openness and attitude toward data privacy leading to the availability of massive datasets usable by its companies are believed to give a significant lead to China in this "race" for the future of artificial intelligence (Zhu et al. 2018; cf. Chapter 5c).

Other countries, meanwhile, are far behind the US and China, but this could change. Let's again have a look at Europe, which currently plays a minor role in artificial intelligence research and development compared to the aforementioned AI superpowers. For now, AI needs big datasets, as it can only be as performant as the size of datasets from which it can learn. The implementation of GDPR across the EU in 2018 certainly slowed down AI's development on the continent, as it places substantial barriers to the storage and handling of (big) data. Yet, also other regions, even AI giant (state of) California, got inspired by GDPR and introduced a similar framework, proof of the recognition of the importance of data security and privacy. Moreover, the need for big data might evolve with AI progress (Nivargi 2020). While an AI system currently needs a few million images to learn how to recognize a cat, children only need a couple of encounters to distinguish cats from dogs. Potentially, future AI will require fewer data, similar to a child's learning process. In that case, big data would be unnecessary and noncritical. In such a new "small data" era, data privacy would likely be highly valued, possibly extending a strong head start to Europe (and California).

It is already clear that international collaboration is needed to prepare societies for AI and ensure worldwide "policies that support the development of beneficial, trustworthy, and robust Artificial Intelligence" (Meltzer and Kerry 2021). Accordingly, the Boston-based Future of Life Institute calls for international cooperation "to guide the safe and beneficial development of AI while reducing race conditions and national and global security threats." International relations and diplomacy should and must avoid the application of artificial intelligence for terrorism and war, but also for tax evasion and economic and industrial espionage, to give just a few examples. Several commensurate guidelines and frameworks have already been discussed and developed by a multitude of supranational organizations. For example, Human Rights Watch and the United Nations regularly call for the drafting of a treaty banning AI-powered arms and weapons (Wareham 2020).

In particular, cultural differences might complicate such international cooperation. While the importance of incorporating ethical guidelines into AI systems has already been underscored, ethics and values differ across cultures. For example, in Hofstede's (1980) cultural dimension framework, China as a highly collectivist culture is likely more open to the sharing of private data if it is for the greater good of the group; whereas the opposite might be the case for highly individualistic countries like the US (Kopalle et al. 2022). This example demonstrates why it might be challenging to find common ground, even between the two AI superpowers. Moreover, Hofstede's uncertainty avoidance can explain cultural differences regarding AI: As a low uncertainty avoidance nation, the US might be less likely to demand strong data protection regulations, while a high uncertainty avoidance culture such as Germany—Europe's strongest economy—might do the opposite. The question to be asked is whether such cultural differences can be overcome. Reports analyzing the convergence of ethical guidelines for AI across various countries indicate that the answer is likely yes. Hagendorff's (2020) report, for example, evaluated more than 20 such ethical guidelines and policies, 80% of which contain requirements for accountability, privacy, and/or fairness. Over two-thirds of them contain recommendations that AI be open, transparent, and sustainable. Nonetheless, over half of them call for human supervision and human control mechanisms (Meltzer and Kerry 2021).

Indeed, a multitude of reports and initiatives exist describing and developing ethical guidelines regarding AI: AlgorithmWatch (2020) identified 166 such initiatives in its AI Ethics Guidelines Global Inventory; and a report by ETH Zurich counted 1,180 codes about ethical guidelines and principles (Jobin, Ienco, and Vayena 2019). Yet, this plethora of reports has a notable shortcoming, as the majority of them focus on and address Western values only. Jobin, Ienco, and Vayena (2019) therefore concluded that the geographical distribution of AI ethics codes is minimal. Over one-third of all guidelines and principles currently originate in the US and the UK. Neither South America nor Africa was represented at all, except within the scope of supranational organizations. Undoubtedly, the Occident is currently taking the lead in the design of AI ethics. Particularly the European Union, as previously mentioned, seems keen on establishing itself as a guarantor for AI ethics. Such an overrepresentation and predominance of the

West contradicts "local knowledge, cultural pluralism, and global fairness" (Jobin, Ienco, and Vayena 2019, p. 396). With China's economic power, its population of over a billion, and its pioneering role in AI development, it appears unlikely that imposing a particular vision of Western values and ethics on the remaining world will lead to a successful outcome. International cooperation to overcome such cultural differences and collaboration among all countries is therefore desirable. In case this is not feasible or remains unattained, one possible outcome might be "AI boxing," or developing several non-connected networks that serve only given regions commensurate with their own principles and guidelines. Unsurprisingly, the three central boxing areas would be led respectively by the US, China, and Europe. AI boxing would be a less-than-ideal solution, however, as trade barriers are hardly a good thing. Moreover, if differing guidelines lead to differing technological standards and infrastructures, it would directly impact business worldwide, and subsequently society in general. Such a scenario definitely appears to be a suboptimal preparation of the global community for the AI (r)evolution (Kaplan and Haenlein 2020).

References

AlgorithmWatch (2020) *AI Ethics Guidelines Global Inventory*. Available at https:// inventory.algorithmwatch.org/database.

Burt, Andrew (2021) New AI Regulations Are Coming: Is Your Organization Ready?, *Harvard Business Review*, April 30.

Dutch Government (2018) *Desinformatie en nepnieuws*. Available at www. rijksoverheid.nl/onderwerpen/desinformatie-nepnieuws.

European Commission (2019) Ethics Guidelines for Trustworthy AI, High-Level Expert Group on Artificial Intelligence, *European Commission*, April 8.

European Commission (2021) Proposal for a Regulation of the European Parliament and the Council Laying Down Harmonized Rules on Artificial Intelligence (Artificial Intelligence Act) and Amending Certain Union Legislative Acts, *European Commission*, April 21.

Hagendorff, Thilo (2020) The Ethics of AI Ethics: An Evaluation of Guidelines, *Minds and Machines*, 30, 99–120.

Hofstede, Geert (1980) *Culture's Consequences: International Differences in Work-Related Values*. London: Sage Publications.

Huang, Ming-Hui, Rust Roland (2018) Artificial Intelligence in Service, *Journal of Service Research*, 21(2), 155–172.

Jobin, Anna, Ienco Marcello, Vayena Effy (2019) The Global Landscape of AI Ethics Guidelines, *Nature Machine Intelligence*, 1.

Kaplan, Andreas (2020) Artificial Intelligence, Social Media, and Fake News: Is This the End of Democracy?, in Gül, A. A., Ertürk, Y. D. and Elmer, P., *Digital Transformation in Media and Society*. Istanbul, Turkey: Istanbul University Press Books, 149–161.

Kaplan, Andreas (2021a) Artificial Intelligence (AI): When Humans and Machines Might Have to Coexist, in Verdegem, P. (ed.), *AI for Everyone? Critical Perspectives*. London: University of Westminster Press, 21–32.

Kaplan, Andreas (2021b) *Higher Education at the Crossroads of Disruption: The University of the 21st Century, Great Debates in Higher Education*. Bingley, UK: Emerald Publishing.

Kaplan, Andreas (2022) *Digital Transformation and Disruption of Higher Education*. Cambridge: Cambridge University Press.

Kaplan, Andreas, Haenlein Michael (2016) Higher Education and the Digital Revolution: About MOOCs, SPOCs, Social Media and the Cookie Monster, *Business Horizons*, 59(4), 441–450.

Kaplan, Andreas, Haenlein Michael (2020) Rulers of the World, Unite! The Challenges and Opportunities of Artificial Intelligence, *Business Horizons*, 63(1), 37–50.

Kim, Hyeongwoo, Garrido Pablo, Tewari Ayush, Xu Weipeng, Thies Justus, Niessner Matthias, Pérez Patrick, Richardt Christian, Zollhöfer Michael, Theobalt Christian (2018) Deep Video Portraits, *ACM Transactions on Graphics*, 37(4).

Kopalle, Praveen, Gangwar Manish, Kaplan Andreas, Ramachandran Divya, Reinartz Werner, Rindfleisch Aric (2022) Examining Artificial Intelligence (AI) Technologies in Marketing Via a Global Lens: Current Trends and Future Research Opportunities, *International Journal of Research in Marketing*, forthcoming.

Meltzer, Joshua P., Kerry Cameron F. (2021) Strengthening International Cooperation on Artificial Intelligence, *Brookings Institution*, February 17.

Nivargi, Vaibhav (2020) The Small Data Revolution: AI Isn't Just for the Big Guys Anymore, *Forbes*, May 19.

Schindler, Philipp (2018) *The Google News Initiative: Building a Stronger Future for News*. Available at www.blog.google/outreach-initiatives/google-news-initiative/announcing-google-news-initiative/.

UNESCO (2019) Planning Education in the AI Era: Lead the Leap, International Conference on Artificial Intelligence and Education, UNESCO, Paris.

Wareham, Mary (2020) Stopping Killer Robots: Country Positions on Banning Fully Autonomous Weapons and Retaining Human Control, *Human Rights Watch*, August 10.

World Economic Forum (2016) The Future of Jobs, Employment, Skills and Workforce Strategy for the Fourth Industrial Revolution, *World Economic Forum*, January.

Zhu, Jun, Huang Tiejun, Chen Wenguagn, Gao Wen (2018) The Future of Artificial Intelligence in China, *Communications of the ACM*, 61(11), 44–45.

5 Cases

From retailing, to retelling, to retaliation

In this chapter, three case studies from differing sectors and of various types will be presented to demonstrate the capability, yet also concern, around artificial intelligence. Several of the aforementioned analyses and ideas will be put into perspective with the help of these cases. We'll begin with Walmart, the US-based retAIl giant, a pioneer in incorporating AI into its activities. Especially during the Covid pandemic, artificial intelligence showed itself to be of immense utility to the Arkansas-based multinational. However, a host of ethical concerns and questions need to be addressed. Next, we'll look at New York's Met, or Metropolitan Museum of ARTificial Intelligence, which is intensively occupied with the use of AI in the culture sector, to give their visitors the opportunity to recount their museum experience on social media. Finally, we'll look at the People's Republic of China, which can be aptly described as the world's AI trAIning field, having successfully incorporated AI into its healthcare sector, to name just one example. Yet, also, the ethics of doing so, that is, controlling and managing the citizenry, will be examined, which in some cases involves state retaliation for citizens' "misdeeds." This explains the chapter's title, "From retailing (Walmart) to retelling (the Met) to retaliation (China)."

a. Walmart: the retAIl giant

Walmart, the world's largest retail chain, which includes discount/big box stores, hypermarkets, and grocery stores, serves over 200 million customers per week, employs approximately two million, and generates more than half a trillion dollars in annual revenues. Throughout Walmart's history, innovation and technology have played a decisive role in its success, beginning with its modest small-town opening in Bentonville, Arkansas, in 1962. Walmart aims to develop new technological applications in record time. For example, its express delivery service, developed during the pandemic, enabling consumers to receive their online purchases in two hours or less

DOI: 10.4324/9781003244554-5

(Perez 2020), took three weeks from idea to pilot. With respect to the utilization of artificial intelligence, Walmart is undeniably one of the pioneers and most active companies in the retail business. Approximately 1,500 data analysts and an additional 50,000 software engineers work for Walmart on thousands of ventures, many involving AI. Therefore, Walmart's case certainly justifies writing "retAIl" [using a capital "A" and "I"] (Kaplan 2020b).

To illustrate one of Walmart's projects, let's look at its inventory management (Perez 2019). AI analyzes in-store camera footage to determine whether restocking shelves is necessary or whether stock needs to be removed, for example perishables having passed their sell-by dates. Artificial intelligence counts the number of items on the shelf, calculates probable demand, forecasts when shoppers are most likely to purchase certain products and whether their purchase will be picked up in-store or delivered, and then proposes commensurate actions. If the store is out of an item, the AI system can order the needed items directly from the supplier. This saves staff a lot of time, which can be shifted to better quality interactions with shoppers, which leads to satisfied customers and a positive effect on retention and satisfaction rates.

Customer satisfaction, one of the main objectives for Walmart implementing technology-based solutions, is furthermore improved with AI-based self-service scales for weighing produce (Chan 2020). Before, shoppers had to click through a list to find the correct product among many, often resulting in annoying waits when a shopper couldn't find the correct item. Now, based on visual recognition, the AI system significantly expedites the weighing process by automatically identifying the fruit or vegetable on the scale, even when merchandise is in layers or bagged.

Again with its customers' shopping experience in mind, Walmart recently filed a patent describing a system able to detect shoppers' emotions via facial recognition and suggesting commensurate actions to be taken by store personnel (Kaplan 2020b). For example, if the AI system identifies a disgruntled-looking customer in the electronics department, a qualified staff member would be dispatched to electronics to assist the shopper. If the system detects not only a single dissatisfied shopper, but rather an entire customer group near the checkout lanes, for example, the likely interpretation would be that the queues are too long. The remedy of opening additional lanes would be immediately advised, thereby reducing wait times to acceptable ones. Walmart stresses the advantages of thus-achieved increased client retention:

> It's easier to retain existing customers than [to] acquire new ones through advertising. Often, if customer service is inadequate, this fact

will not appear in data available to management until many customers have been lost. With so much competition, a customer will often simply go elsewhere rather than take the time to make a complaint.

(Nassauer 2017)

Moreover, long-term buying behavior and future shopping trends could be AI-calculated by analyzing a combination of customers' emotions, in-store shopper tracking, and shoppers' transactional data (Peterson 2017).

Another area wherein Walmart uses AI is in its negotiations with its suppliers (Banker 2021). Interacting with an AI-powered chatbot step by step, suppliers reveal their willingness-to-pay and pain points. The AI system applies a series of negotiation tactics and strategies, such as mirroring back a supplier's response, thus ensuring that s/he feels understood, with the objective of finding the optimal deal for Walmart while at the same time not frustrating the negotiating party. Constantly improving, the system autonomously learns how suppliers negotiate and what their various strategies are, thus getting better each time it engages in a negotiation. Numbers indicate that Walmart improved its profitability between 2.8% and 6.8% (Kahn 2021). Obviously such a human /machine interface also comes with drawbacks, such as several suppliers not feeling appreciated facing a chatbot, but overall, Walmart's experience and results thus far are promising.

Finally, during the Covid-19 pandemic, AI helped Walmart to adapt to new customer demands such as shortening turnaround times for home deliveries. As soon as an online shopper puts her first item in her cart, the AI system begins determining whether this customer can be provided with a delivery in two hours or less. Calculations are based on a variety of data points such as the total number of items, location (both the delivery address and the locale where the order was made), availability of stock and staff, and traffic and weather conditions. Similar computations are done concerning Walmart's return policy. Just as online purchases significantly increased during the pandemic, the number of returns also increased. Having to return items not only creates frustration among clients, but it also adds cost to the retailer having to receive the product, repackage it, and resell it, if indeed the merchandise is resellable. In Walmart's case, AI-driven calculations take into account an item's price, the processing cost for the (potentially) returned product, the client's purchasing history, and her customer loyalty rating. If reselling is ruled out, Walmart prefers to offer the client to keep the item free of charge and issue a new command.

Also during the pandemic, AI proved its usefulness as an effective promotion tool. To deal with the influx in online purchases, Walmart had to hire no less than half a million new employees and promoted 200,000 of its current workforce (Zielinski 2020). To do so as quickly as possible, artificial intelligence was used to forecast an employee's likely performance, retention potential, and resulting financial impact. David Futrell, one of Walmart's senior human resources directors, estimated the return-on-investment of this AI system at millions of dollars, stating that even moderate forecasts "showed savings in the hundreds of millions annually. This estimate only includes eliminating replacement costs of (not) hiring the lowest-scoring candidates. If we included estimates of lost productivity and training costs, the real impact might exceed $1 billion annually" (Futrell and Allen 2020). Most likely, this system will also pay for itself many times over in the aftermath of Covid-19.

Although Walmart specifies that information is stored for less than one week, the application of AI technology in the retail sector raises a set of ethical concerns: Does Walmart, or does the client, own a given client's information on purchasing behavior? Would Walmart be allowed to sell such data to suppliers or other third parties (depending on the store's country location)? Who would be accountable and responsible in the event that biased AI repeatedly suggests the checking of pockets of darker-complected shoppers? For the moment, AI systems free up time for Walmart employees who are transferred to higher-value activities. Will this continue? Or might these employees be replaced entirely by AI-driven machines and robots? Currently, Walmart uses AI-driven chatbots for its negotiations with suppliers. Suppose suppliers also begin using AI. Might the future be characterized by machines negotiating with other machines?

b. New York's Metropolitan Museum of ARTificial intelligence

New York City's Metropolitan Museum of Art, more familiarly called "the Met," is the largest art museum in the US. Its permanent collection contains over two million pieces, divided into 17 wings. The collection contains works from ancient Egypt, classical antiquity, pieces by all major European painters, and of course an impressive collection of American art and artists, among much more. Consistently very open to technological progress, the Met follows an open-access policy: Several hundred thousand high-resolution images of its art pieces are allowed to be shared and used online, free of any copyright charges, which strongly benefits their diffusion on Wikipedia and other sites (Kaplan and Haenlein 2014). Making ample use of artificial intelligence within a multitude of current and planned activities, the Met could therefore justifiably be called the Metropolitan Museum of ARTificial Intelligence (Kaplan 2020b, 2020c).

To merit this rebranding, the Met has begun a collaboration with Microsoft and the Massachusetts Institute of Technology (MIT): the Met x Microsoft

x MIT initiative. Its objective is mainly to augment visitor engagement with the art and the museum itself, but also to invent innovative and creative communication means enabling visitors to retell their museum adventures on their social media platforms (Kessler 2019). Mitra Azizirad, one of Microsoft's vice presidents in charge of artificial intelligence, said, "The close partnership between the Met, MIT, and Microsoft is a great example of how AI is empowering curators and technologists to make art and human history accessible and relevant to everyone on the planet" (The Met 2019). Following are a few of the venture's projects, initiated during a two-day hackathon (Kaplan 2020b):

- Storyteller: AI-driven voice recognition follows visitors' discussions with their companions while walking through the museum. Subsequently, the AI system suggests paintings and other art that fit the visitor's conversational topics. Moreover, the system is able to provide the perfect suggestion for an entire museum tour based on these listened-into conversations. A visitor's engagement most likely would be increased, with her telling about her visit and tour on social media. Even an entire, ready-to-print art catalogue will be provided by the AI system based on visitors' conversations. By the way, Storyteller is able to pick up conversations in over 64 languages.
- Tag, That's It!: This project actually could be described as transforming visitors into museum staff in disguise. Via an app, visitors can tag images of the art whimsically. Through gamification, the museum's employee, aka visitor, is incentivized to tag images they take during their visit and to describe them in as much detail as possible. This way, databases are created containing valuable information about the Met's collection, which is of great value to adding to the existing corpus of art knowledge.
- Artwork of the Day: This project describes an AI system which, by considering current events, that day's headlines, a visitor's location and historical behavior, and weather conditions and forecasts, suggests to each visitor her personalized and customized artwork of the day, that is, each visitor obtains an individual suggestion for an artwork of particular appeal and interest given her personal circumstances and matters that are of current significance to her. Furthermore, the system promises that no two visitors will get the same artwork suggestion on a given day; not only is the visitor's experience ultra-personal, but the system also prevents crowding.
- My Life, My Met: This project proposes screening visitors' social media feeds and subsequently suggesting artworks that are similar to images on their social media (Kaplan and Haenlein 2010; Kaplan 2012). For

example, a photo of a visitor at a music festival could "become" an ancient painting of some feast at an imperial court. The assumption is that such images would be heavily shared with a visitor's followers on social media. Therefore, this project would constitute a perfect promotional channel, bringing authentic art into the lives of thousands of teenagers and young and not-so-young adults.

• Gen Studio: This project enables a visitor to understand the shared characteristics and elements underlying all of the Met's collection. Via AI, the visitor iterates between various art pieces that are linked in new ways based on their materials, forms, and styles. Gen Studio thus can be considered a precursor project of MosAIc, an algorithm developed at MIT's Computer Science and Artificial Intelligence Laboratory (Adams 2020). With an almost infinite number of artworks, even the most knowledgeable expert would find it nearly impossible to find all of the connections between pieces from various locations and time periods. Similar to Gen Studio, AI-driven MosAIc helps in this endeavor by expanding its reach to Amsterdam's Rijksmuseum and detecting thus far unknown links between paintings of both museums. Similarities are not limited to visuals only, but are also found for themes, motifs, and overall meaning. The aim is to gain new insights into art history, as well as civilization's evolution in general.

The Covid-19 pandemic obviously accentuated and accelerated the application of AI and new technologies to the world of culture, with most museums forced into lockdown and closed to the public for months. The Met as well tried to bring its cultural experience into people's living rooms via digital means. Partnering with telecommunications provider Verizon, the Met applied augmented as well as virtual reality. This virtual exhibition, titled Unframed, enabled visitors to virtually explore the museum's collection with an astonishing degree of realism. Augmented reality included animations that appeared real, as well as a series of games, keeping housebound visitors entertained (Zelaya 2021).

The Met's use of AI raises several questions: Might there be concerns about privacy and personal data? Sharing one's conversations during a museum visit might result in an interesting walk-through, but will visitors be able to control what they said, and will they be aware of their being listened to while in the museum? Supposing highly personal and potentially harmful information is shared while doing so? Who is accountable in case such shared information leads to negative outcomes? Is it ethical to ask museum visitors to do the work, that is, tagging artworks, instead of the museum itself? Might artificial intelligence systems become future artists and replace human creators? What actually is creativity, and will it be possible to distinguish machine-produced art from human-produced art?

c. China: the ultimate AI trAIning ground

In July 2017, the Chinese government announced its New Generation Artificial Intelligence Development Plan, codifying its ambitions to world leadership in AI by 2030 (Mozur 2017). Former Google CEO Eric Schmidt predicted that China could overtake the US in artificial intelligence even sooner (Ponciano 2021); others would say that China already leads in AI. Regardless, to reach this goal, China is developing a powerful ecosystem bringing together academia, private and public players, and capital, as well as AI expertise, talent, and big data (Kaplan 2021a, 2020a). Specifically concerning the latter, the Chinese government expanded connections between authorities and the workplace for facilitating the collection, assessment, and application of data. China's large population, centralized government, and minimal data protection and privacy laws are particularly beneficial to AI advancement, whose success depends heavily on learning from very large datasets. This environment extends China a significant edge. Estimations state that China might dispose of nearly one-third of worldwide available data by 2030. Take Didi, China's version of Uber. With more than half a billion passengers, Didi collects and processes approximately 70 terabytes of data daily from approximately 1,000 ride requests *per second* (Li, Tong, and Xiao 2021).

China's up-and-coming AI workforce is trained in thousands of new programs launched at universities nationwide, which has opened up hundreds of new positions for professors specializing in AI-related fields. This strategy has borne fruit, as by now, China has the highest publication output focusing on artificial intelligence: While in 1997, China's share of publications in AI globally was around 4%, only two decades later it approaches 30% (Li, Tong, and Xiao 2021). And in case local talent sourcing is not enough, China is equally keen on attracting talent from abroad. As the largest capital market for AI startups, China supports a dynamic entrepreneurial scene while ensuring companies' growth and scale-up. Moreover, organizations are strongly encouraged to collaborate: Even the three Chinese tech giants Alibaba, Baidu, and Tencent are asked to share and exchange their data with each other, leading to immense datasets. Such data sharing helps Chinese companies to rapidly bring new AI-powered products and services to the market. Furthermore, the Chinese are eager users of new technology and relatively early adopters of AI. All this enables fast refinement and improvement of newly launched AI-driven offerings (Westerheide 2020).

An exemplary area wherein China strongly and successfully applies AI is in healthcare, which is particularly under pressure due to a shortage of medical professionals and an increasingly aging population. Artificial intelligence provides the possibility of delivering customized healthcare at relatively low cost facilitated by AI-driven chatbots to detect (potential) illnesses at early stages through continuous monitoring, thereby reducing the need for (human) medical staff, to speed up the development of new medications, and more. In February 2021, for example, Chinese scientists confirmed that their AI was capable of identifying broadly spread childhood diseases with similar precision than that accomplished by pediatricians. Their dataset comprised 600,000 children all having been patients at the same hospital, data quantity that most other countries can only dream of (O'Meara 2019). More recently, China also proved AI to be efficient in its battle against COVID-19: Medical imaging technology was applied to detect COVID-19 cases as fast as possible, AI-based surveillance systems remotely monitored patients, and AI-powered robots reduced the risk of virus exposure by enabling, for example, contactless meal delivery in hospitals (Candelon, Gombe, and Khodabandeh 2021).

AI-based surveillance systems are used not only in Chinese healthcare, but also to control and monitor society at large. What might very well seem to be a page taken straight from *1984*, George Orwell's famous dystopia, is reality in China: A machine controls and guides society. A machine judges good or bad behavior. A machine determines compensation or fines. China's AI-driven social score program collects various information on its citizens, assigning each a certain score based on her behavior, which then determines that citizen's options (Creemers 2018). This might sound similar to banks checking an applicant's credibility prior to extending (or refusing to extend) a loan. In Germany, for example, such credit checks are performed by the Schufa, the General Credit Protection Agency, a private credit bureau. In the same vein, eBay and many used booksellers apply vendor ratings based on the vendor's communication/response times, shipping times, and product quality. Airbnb rates guests as well as hosts, and Uber passengers and drivers rate each other. Despite potential similarities, however, the latter examples describe time-sensitive and limited scoring systems, whereas China's system embodies a holistic approach: Mass surveillance is enabled via millions of security cameras nationwide equipped with high-performance facial recognition using a database including nearly every member of China's 1.4 billion-strong population.

Within China's scoring program, points can be won, for example, for paying bills on time, consistent safe driving, donating blood, or publicly praising the government. Demerits, on the contrary, are collected for criticizing the state on social media or engaging in fraudulent behavior, in addition to lesser offenses such as sticking chewing gum under a subway seat, smoking in non-smoking areas, playing loud music, being a no-show at a restaurant, or purchasing too many video games. Good social scores enable more freedom to travel, discounts on a variety of products and services, priority treatment at governmental agencies, better loan terms, faster promotion in the workplace, and more. Bad scores lead to the opposite outcomes and may even result in children of low-scoring citizens to be blocked from enrolling in university. Bad scores can be improved by engaging in community service to regain points. China applies social scoring not only to citizens, but also to businesses to ensure compliance with regulations and overall accountability. Good business scores then lead to positive credit evaluations, more investment possibilities, and lower taxes. Conversely, bad scores result in difficulties when applying for loans, higher taxes, and fewer opportunities to be considered for state-financed ventures and programs.

China's AI application in its health sector as well as for architecture of an Orwellian authoritarian state illustrate both sides of the AI coin. We thus can legitimately ask whether China deserves the title of AI pioneer or AI villain. To be fair, China is by far not the only country using artificial intelligence for dubious purposes. Singapore, for example, is working on a similar AI-powered monitoring system for its citizens. Regardless of whether this is pioneering or totalitarian, one thing is certain: China has become the world's trAIning ground in artificial intelligence. Several additional questions therefore arise: What could China's predominance in AI mean for the world's economy? Are there geopolitical consequences thereto? How high would we estimate the risk (if any), and what potential security measures are at our disposal? Is social scoring ethical? Might it be ethical within the scope of Chinese culture versus that of the West?

References

Adams, Dallon R. (2020) MIT and Microsoft Algorithm Determines Correlations in Vast Art Collections, *TechRepublic*, July 29.

Banker, Steve (2021) Walmart's Massive Investment in a Supply Chain Transformation, *Forbes*, April 23.

Candelon, Francois, Gombeaud Matthieu, Khodabandeh Shervin (2021) China's Response to COVID Showed the World How to Make the Most of A.I., *Fortune*, June 4.

Chan, Jenny (2020) Self-Service Scales in Walmart Never the Same again after Covid19, *Medium*, April 28.

Creemers, Rogier (2018) China's Social Credit System: An Evolving Practice of Control, SSRN.

Futrell, David, Allen Josh (2020) High-Velocity Selection: Predicting Performance and Retention at Walmart, *SIOP*, October 6.

Kahn, Jeremy (2021) This A.I. Startup Is Saving Walmart and Other Big Companies Millions by Automating Negotiations, *Fortune*, April 27.

Kaplan, Andreas (2012) If You Love Something, Let It Go Mobile: Mobile Marketing and Mobile Social Media 4×4, *Business Horizons*, 55(2), 129–139.

Kaplan, Andreas (2020a) Artificial Intelligence, Social Media, and Fake News: Is This the End of Democracy?, in Gül, A. A., Ertürk, Y. D. and Elmer, P. (eds.), *Digital Transformation in Media and Society*. Istanbul, Turkey: Istanbul University Press Books, 149–161.

Kaplan, Andreas (2020b) Artificial Intelligence, Marketing, and the Fourth Industrial Revolution: Clarifications, Challenges, Concerns, in Christiansen, B. and Škrinjarić, T. (eds.), *Handbook of Research on Applied AI for International Business and Marketing Applications*. Hershey, Pennsylvania: IGI, 1–13.

Kaplan, Andreas (2020c) Marrying Cultural Heritage and High Tech: The Use of ARTificial Intelligence in Museums (Beijing's Palace Museum, NYC's Met, and Paris' Louvre), The Case Centre, Case 320–0057–1.

Kaplan, Andreas (2021a) Artificial Intelligence (AI): When Humans and Machines Might Have to Coexist, in Verdegem, P. (ed.), *AI for Everyone? Critical Perspectives*. London: University of Westminster Press, 21–32.

Kaplan, Andreas, Haenlein Michael (2010) Users of the World, Unite! The Challenges and Opportunities of Social Media, *Business Horizons*, 53(1), 59–68.

Kaplan, Andreas, Haenlein Michael (2014) Collaborative Projects (Social Media Application): About Wikipedia, the Free Encyclopedia, *Business Horizons*, 57(5), 617–626.

Kessler, Maria (2019) The Met x Microsoft x MIT: A Closer Look at the Collaboration, *The Met*, February 21.

Li, Daitan, Tong Tony W., Xiao Yangao (2021) Is China Emerging as the Global Leader in AI?, *Harvard Business Review*, February 18.

The Met (2019) The Met, Microsoft, and MIT Explore the Impact of Artificial Intelligence on How Global Audiences Connect with Art, February 4.

Mozur, Paul (2017) Beijing Wants A.I. to Be Made in China by 2030, *The New York Times*, July 20.

Nassauer, Sarah (2017) Robots Are Replacing Workers Where You Shop: Wal-Mart and Other Large Retailers, under Pressure from Amazon, Turn to Technology to Do Workers' Rote Tasks, *Wall Street Journal*, July 19.

O'Meara, Sarah (2019) Will China Lead the World in AI by 2030?, *Nature*, August 21.

Perez, Sarah (2019) Walmart Unveils an AI-Powered Store of the Future, Now Open to the Public, *Tech Crunch*, April 25.

Perez, Sarah (2020) Walmart Is Piloting a Pricier 2-Hour Express Grocery Delivery Service, *Tech Crunch*, April 30.

Peterson, Hayley (2017) Walmart Is Developing a Robot That Identifies Unhappy Shoppers, *Business Insider*, July 19.

Ponciano, Jonathan (2021) Google Billionaire Eric Schmidt Warns of 'National Emergency' If China Overtakes U.S. in AI Tech, *Forbes*, April 7.

Westerheide, Fabian (2020) China: The First Artificial Intelligence Superpower, *Forbes*, January 14.

Zelaya, Ian (2021) This Verizon-Powered Virtual Art Experience Brings the Met to You, *Adweek*, January 1.

Zielinski, Dave (2020) Delta Air Lines, Walmart Use HR Technology to Stay Agile during COVID-19 Pandemic, *SHRM*, December 1.

6 Conclusions
Our fate made in machines

We've decrypted and illustrated artificial intelligence and presented its good and bad sides currently and in the (likely) future. What remains is to ask whether humanity's fate will indeed be sealed by and made in machines. The introduction mentioned concerns thereabout expressed by Elon Musk and Stephen Hawking (2014), the latter moreover having said in an interview with the BBC that artificial intelligence "could spell the end of the human race." Entrepreneur and inventor Clive Sinclair (2014), for his part, also in a BBC interview, paraphrased AI's danger thusly: "Once you start to make machines that are rivaling and surpassing humans with intelligence, it's going to be very difficult for us to survive." Finally, the University of Oxford's Future of Humanity Institute, which studies the threats that could destroy human civilization, has placed AI at the top of its agenda. Might AI indeed mean the end of human civilization?

Theoretically, the scenario of humanity disappearing due to the advent of artificial superintelligence can be summarized under the term "existential risk," that is, substantial advances in AI will lead to the extinction of human beings or some other irreparable disaster on a global level (Bostrom 2002, 2014; Russel and Norvig 2009). The main argument therefore overturns the claim that humans currently control other living species due to our superior intelligence, that is, if a machine surpasses humans in intelligence, the same reasoning—devices controlling humans—applies. Several explanations of why and how such a takeover of machines from humans exist.

First, we humans could easily be taken by surprise with AI-driven machines and robots rapidly and exponentially increasing their intelligence—also called "the intelligence explosion"—which would lead to our simply losing control (Good 1965). Second, it might be impossible to provide machines with human values, without which human extinction would become more likely. As discussed in Chapter 4, even seemingly harmless AI could misinterpret a given goal and unintentionally act detrimentally. Imagine an AI system tasked with pursuing Earth's sustainability: It could simply decide

DOI: 10.4324/9781003244554-6

to eradicate humans as the primary source of pollution and global warming. In such a case, many researchers strongly doubt that an AI system could quickly be turned off or have its goals changed without resistance. This phenomenon is described as "instrumental convergence," that is, the hypothetical impulse of sufficiently intelligent actors to aspire to potentially boundless instrumental aims given that their ultimate objectives are themselves limitless (Bostrom 2014).

Human extinction, however, does not even need AI systems to intentionally or unintentionally be executed; humanity might do so on our own. To illustrate such a scenario, let's look at Neal Stephenson's (1992) novel *Snow Crash*, wherein the protagonist, Hiroaki, spends most of his time in a virtual environment (Haenlein and Kaplan 2009; Kaplan and Haenlein 2009a, 2009b, 2009c, 2009d), the Metaverse, where one can, for example, visit museums, dance in nightclubs, make friends, or consume virtual narcotics, such as the pseudo-drug snow crash, which gives the book its title. To access the Metaverse and transform into one's avatar, users need only a computer and a pair of goggles. To some humans, the Metaverse is preferable to their real lives, so they decide to permanently live as their avatars, remaining indoors, with only the hardware needed to access and remain in the AI-driven virtual world. In such a setting, human reproduction is unlikely, naturally leading to the species' extinction.

While Neal Stephenson's Metaverse and its potential appeal seem unrealistic at first glance, research shows that mice (and humans) with electrodes implanted into their brains' pleasure centers rapidly become addicted to the pleasure bursts, and consequently stimulate themselves as often as possible. Additionally, think of the time some of us spend playing video games, in many cases getting addicted, which can lead to exhaustion and ultimately death. Furthermore, research on virtual worlds such as Second Life shows that a significant portion of users feel these worlds to be an extension of their real lives, preferring their "second life" over their "first" (Kaplan 2009; Kaplan and Haenlein 2010). Add to this the possibility that many people might no longer be employed or employable, as AI and automation take over their work. Finally, we have Elon Musk's recent startup, Neuralink, which develops brain implants to achieve perfect fusion between artificial and human intelligence. Combine all this, and the Metaverse appears to be closer than we think.

We indeed can and should ask ourselves how likely such doomsday scenarios are, and whether we should be worried about taking accordant action. While current AI evolution indicates that there is no risk of AI attaining superintelligence soon, or ever, there's a saying in the world of technology, oft-quoted by Bill Gates, that people "always overestimate the change that will occur in the next two years, and underestimate the change that will occur in the next ten" (Gates 1996). The improbability of a nuclear power plant exploding avoided neither Chernobyl nor Fukushima. Ultimately, this would be a reinterpretation of 17th-century French mathematician, philosopher, physicist, and theologian Blaise Pascal's theory that "it is worth behaving as if God existed" (Pascal and Lafuma 1962). This theory, also called Pascal's wager, posits that in case God does not actually exist, an individual acting as per God's laws would only lose out on some relatively minor pleasures (finite loss); while if God does exist, this individual would reap infinite benefits (such as eternal life in heaven) and escape eternal suffering. If an event, even if highly improbable, might lead to a terrible outcome, it might therefore be worth reconsidering it.

Final food for thought is provided by Max Tegmark (2018) in his book *Life 3.0: Being Human in the Age of Artificial Intelligence*, wherein Tegmark looks at various definitions of life, noting that doing so is notoriously difficult. Some (narrow) definitions of life require particular parameters, such as cell composition. Others define life more broadly as a process capable of retaining its complexity and replication. While the narrow definition excludes AI as life, the broad definition leaves room for interpretation. Currently, we can already implant artificial organs and bones. Suppose that, in the future, AI can directly enhance one's brainpower, or physical performance. As per Tegmark, life needs to undergo its final upgrade, that is, to Life 3.0, or be the master of its own fate, free of biological limitations. Pushed to its limits, we can ask whether there is still any difference between an AI-powered robot or the enhanced "human" à la the 1970s' TV series *Six Million Dollar Man*, about a former astronaut who, in the aftermath of a NASA flight crash, is entirely reconstructed with superhuman vision, speed, and strength via bionic implants and is subsequently hired as a US government secret agent. So ultimately, it might indeed all be a question of religious or philosophical beliefs about what human life is or should be, bringing us back to Pascal's wager. Reader, what do you wager?

References

Bostrom, Nick (2002) Existential Risks, *Journal of Evolution and Technology*, 9(1), 1–31.

Bostrom, Nick (2014) *Superintelligence: Paths, Dangers, Strategies*. Oxford: Oxford University Press.

Gates, Bill (1996) *The Road Ahead*. New York, US: Penguin Books.

Good, Irving J. (1965) Speculations Concerning the First Ultraintelligent Machine, *Advances in Computers*, 6, 31–33.

Haenlein, Michael, Kaplan Andreas (2009) Flagship Brand Stores within Virtual Worlds: The Impact of Virtual Store Exposure on Real Life Band Attitudes and Purchase Intent, *Recherche et Applications en Marketing*, 24(3), 57–80.

Hawking, Stephen (2014) Stephen Hawking: 'AI Could Spell End of the Human Race', Interview, BBC, December 2.

Kaplan, Andreas (2009) Second Life: Leçons pour le monde réel, *Expansion Management Review*, 133(Juin), 58–60.

Kaplan, Andreas, Haenlein Michael (2009a) Consumer Use and Business Potential of Virtual Worlds: The Case of Second Life, *International Journal on Media Management*, 11(3/4), 93–101.

Kaplan, Andreas, Haenlein Michael (2009b) Consumers, Companies and Virtual Social Worlds: A Qualitative Analysis of Second Life, *Advances in Consumer Research*, 36(1), 873–874.

Kaplan, Andreas, Haenlein Michael (2009c) The Fairyland of Second Life: About Virtual Social Worlds and How to Use Them, *Business Horizons*, 52(6), 563–572.

Kaplan, Andreas, Haenlein Michael (2009d) Utilisation et potentiel commercial des hyperréalités: Une analyse qualitative de Second Life, *Revue Francaise du Marketing*, 222(Mai), 69–81.

Kaplan, Andreas, Haenlein Michael (2010) Mondes virtuels: retour au réalisme, *Expansion Management Review*, 138(Septembre), 90–102.

Pascal, Blaise, Lafuma Louis (1962) *Pensées*. Paris, France: Seuil.

Russell, Stuart, Norvig Peter (2009) 26.3: The Ethics and Risks of Developing Artificial Intelligence, Artificial Intelligence: A Modern Approach, Prentice Hall.

Sinclair, Clive (2014) Sir Clive Sinclair on Personal Computing, Interview, BBC.

Stephenson, Neal (1992) *Snow Crash*. New York, US: Bantam Books.

Tegmark, Max (2018) *Life 3.0: Being Human in the Age of Artificial Intelligence*. London, UK: Penguin Books Ltd.

Index

Printed and bound by CPI Group (UK) Ltd, Croydon, CR0 4YY

17/10/2024

01775689-0008